ENGLISH
FOR
LIFE
THROUGH
PICTURES

TERRY BRAY

Bilingual Program
Shared Lit. Collection

Dominie Press, Inc.

Publisher: Raymond Yuen
Executive Editor: Carlos Byfield
Editor: Karen Hannabarger
Cover Designer: Tyler Blik
Text Designer: Kristi Mendola
Illustrator: Kathleen Robb Parks

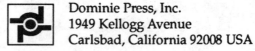 Dominie Press, Inc.
1949 Kellogg Avenue
Carlsbad, California 92008 USA

ISBN 1-56270-009-X

Printed in U.S.A.

3 4 5 6 7 8 9 10 W 99 98 97

Contents

Introduction

English for Life through Pictures is intended for use by young adult and adult students who have a very basic knowledge of English. It is designed for ESL students who are living in North America and are continuously exposed to its lifestyle. The lessons lead students from the beginning level to the intermediate level and expose them to meaningful listening, reading, writing, and speaking activities.

The text can be used in small groups, large groups, or with individuals. It is suitable for use in multilevel or homogenous classrooms.

Each of the eight units comprises four short lessons. Each lesson includes the following sections:

- Presentation — suggested scenario for the illustrations.

- Controlled Practice — pair work in which one partner completes and asks questions and the other answers.

- Comprehension — varied format. Each unit contains true/false or true/false/maybe exercises, contradicting answers to questions, completion of sentences, or provision of the second line of a dialogue.

- Descriptive Phase — questions based on the author's suggested scenario.

- Role Play — pair work in which students choose a partner and a role. Each partner has an opportunity to play the other's role. The language used is colloquial.

- Pair/Group Work — questions based on a topic personalized for students. Students must apply content to their individual situations.

English for Life through Pictures is based on the premise that language acquisition is accomplished in the duality of classroom interaction and real-life exposure. The more closely related the classroom situation is to the students' needs in the real world, the more meaningful and functional the language becomes. As language becomes more meaningful and concrete, acquisition becomes more expedient. The more physically and mentally involved a student becomes, the better he or she will acquire the language.

Each lesson conveys a real-life situation through a set of sequenced illustrations followed by pragmatic learning activities. These provide students with a meaningful context from which to acquire language that they can use in everyday situations. As a result students are exposed to what they need to understand and express, and the structures they must have to produce more language.

Competencies, functions, and grammar are introduced by getting students involved with topics that are interesting and relevant to their needs. The content is presented in such a way that students feel encouraged and successful in their attempts to communicate meaningfully. The lessons build students' confidence by supplying them with the language necessary to function successfully outside the classroom, while providing them with the comfort and security of practicing and learning in a non-stressful environment with their peers.

English for Life through Pictures emphasizes comprehension and communication, while presenting opportunities for the implementation of cooperative learning exercises. Cooperative learning enhances comprehension as well as production of language. The probability of language acquisition increases as input is made more comprehensible.

Non-English speakers need to understand messages and express themselves in order to function successfully in North America. This text introduces language in such a way that students learn to comprehend and react to messages in a culturally sensitive manner.

Notes to the Teacher

BEFORE YOU BEGIN

Look over the lesson you want to teach and gather any props that might serve as visual aids for the picture story. Then, read through the presentation and familiarize yourself with the text of the lesson.

If possible, make an overhead transparency of the picture story and have an overhead projector ready. Ask the students to close all books and notebooks and to put their pens and pencils down. They will only look, listen, speak, and act out the lesson at first.

If an overhead projector is not available, have students look at the pictures in their books.

TEACHING THE STORY

Ask students to tell you the names of different items in the first picture. Read the first sentence of the presentation and allow them to listen. Act out the picture, if possible, and repeat the sentence several times. Encourage the students to act out the pictures with you. When you feel they understand what is going on, ask some comprehension questions about the pictures.

When you are ready, move on to the next picture and proceed in the same way.

After all the pictures have been done, dictate the story to higher level students. For lower level students, elicit the story back from them and write it on the board. Select volunteers to read the story from the board and to monitor pronunciation.

Use the following guidelines as necessary to help students gain a better understanding of the story:

- Ask comprehension questions about each picture.

- Change the tense of each story to past or future.

- Change the names to pronouns.

- Add time words such as today, yesterday, tomorrow, right now, etc.

- Allow students to make up their own stories, using some or all of the pictures.

- Mix up the pictures or presentation and have the students unscramble them and put them in the right order.

- Pair the students and have them tell each other the story using only the pictures.

- Make a cloze exercise out of the presentation and have the students fill in the blanks as you read the story.

- Read sentences randomly from the presentation and ask students to point out the corresponding pictures.
- Role play the story using props and the dialogues.

USING THE EXERCISES

Do the exercises after the picture story has been taught. They can be done as pair or group work, in class or at home. However, they should always be checked and corrected as a group in the classroom.

Presentation

After you have taught the story, read the story lines randomly and ask students to identify the illustration that each line describes.

Have the students read the sentences silently. Then, select several of the easiest sentences and dictate them to the students.

The sentences may be assigned ahead of time as a reading assignment. They may also be used as a base from which you may ask the students to change tenses and noun phrases.

Controlled Practice

Be sure that students know how to ask and answer questions prior to completing this section.

Pair the students and ask them to work together to fill in the missing words. Encourage this to be a conversational exchange in which each student listens to the other and then fills in the correct words.

Accept short answers as given and complete answers.

Comprehension

Do the exercises in this section as group exercises.

For the true/false and true/false/maybe exercises, have students read the statements. Then, let students vote as a group on whether the statements are true, false, or maybe could be true.

The statements in the contradiction exercises are false. Have students contradict these statements following the form of the first answer, which is given. More ambitious students may be encouraged to give a more complete answer.

Descriptive Phase

Have students use one word answers, phrases, or full length sentences, depending on their abilities. These can be done in conjunction with looking at the pictures or with a reading of the presentation.

Role Play

Set this up as a pair practice. Students comfortable with speaking in front of the class can be given the necessary props and asked to act out the scenes.

Pair/Group Work

Do this as a survey. Have students ask the questions to their partners or group and then report their findings to the whole class.

Do You Have a Problem?

A Fire

Look at the illustrations. Listen carefully to your teacher.

1

1. Luis is in his living room watching TV.
2. He smells smoke.
3. He runs into his children's room and wakes them.
4. They get down on their hands and knees.
5. They crawl out the front door.
6. They run over to their neighbor's house.
7. Luis knocks on the door and his neighbor answers.
8. Luis points at the fire.
9. The neighbor calls the fire department.

CONTROLLED PRACTICE
*Work with a partner.
One partner completes and
asks the questions. The other
partner answers.*

1. What is Luis _____ in his living room?
   _____ watching TV.
2. What _____ he smell?
   _____ smoke.
3. _____ does he run?
   _____ into his children's room.
4. What _____ they do?
   _____ get down on their hands and knees.
5. Where do _____ crawl?
   _____ out the front door.
6. Where do they _____ ?
   _____ to their neighbor's house.
7. _____ knocks on the door?
   Luis _____ .
8. What does Luis _____ ?
   He _____ at the fire.
9. Who _____ the neighbor call?
   _____ the fire department.

COMPREHENSION
*Read the sentences. Then, write
true or false on the lines.*

_____ 1. Luis is sleeping in his living room.

_____ 2. There's a fire at Luis' neighbor's house.

_____ 3. Luis and his children crawl out the back door.

_____ 4. Luis' neighbor is home.

_____ 5. Luis' neighbor doesn't call the fire department.

DESCRIPTIVE PHASE

Answer the following questions.

1. Where are Luis' children?
2. What are they doing?
3. Who knocks on the neighbor's door?
4. Who calls the fire department?

ROLE PLAY

Work with a partner. You play one role. Your partner plays the other role. Then, switch roles.

Andres:	Hello, my house is on fire, hurry!
Firefighter:	Slow down, take a deep breath.
Andres:	Sorry, I'm okay now.
Firefighter:	Is everyone out of your house?
Andres:	Yes, we're all out.
Firefighter:	Okay, what's your address?
Andres:	10339 Mildred Avenue, Covina.
Firefighter:	Okay, a truck is on its way.
Andres:	Thank you. Please hurry.
Firefighter:	We will. Keep everybody away from the house.

PAIR/GROUP WORK

Ask your partner or group the following questions.

1. Do you have fire extinguishers in your house or apartment?
2. Where are the smoke alarms in your house or apartment?
3. Are there fire extinguishers at your school? Where?
4. Your clothes are on fire. What do you do?
5. Your house is on fire. There's a lot of smoke. What do you do?
6. What number do you dial for the fire department?

A Prowler

Look at the illustrations. Listen carefully to your teacher.

PRESENTATION
Read the following sentences.

1. Alfredo and his wife are sleeping.
2. A prowler breaks into their house through a window.
3. The prowler knocks over a lamp.
4. Alfredo and his wife wake up.
5. Alfredo picks up the phone and calls the police.
6. He tells the police that there's someone downstairs.
7. The police send a car over to Alfredo's house right away.
8. The police car shines its light on the house.
9. The prowler jumps out the back window.

CONTROLLED PRACTICE
Work with a partner. One partner completes and asks the questions. The other partner answers.

1. What _____ Alfredo and his wife doing?
   _____ sleeping.
2. Who _____ their house through a window?
   A prowler _____ .
3. What does the _____ knock over?
   _____ a lamp.
4. Who _____ up?
   Alfredo and his wife _____ .
5. Who does Alfredo _____ ?
   _____ the police.
6. What does he _____ the police?
   _____ that there's someone downstairs.
7. When do the police _____ a car over to Alfredo's house?
   _____ right away.
8. _____ does the police car shine its light?
   _____ on the house.
9. Who _____ out the back window?
   The prowler _____ .

COMPREHENSION
Complete the second line of these dialogues.

1. Alfredo: There's someone in the house.
   Dolores: *Let's call 911.*

2. Alfredo: Is that the number for emergencies?
   Dolores: _____

3. Alfredo: What did they say?
   Dolores: _____

4. Alfredo: Where's the prowler now?
   Dolores: _____

DESCRIPTIVE PHASE
Answer the following questions.

1. How does the prowler get into Alfredo's house?
2. How many prowlers are there?
3. Why do Alfredo and his wife wake up?
4. Who calls the police?
5. Who shines a light on Alfredo's house?
6. Why does the prowler jump out the back window?

ROLE PLAY
Work with a partner. You play one role. Your partner plays the other role. Then, switch roles.

Alfredo: Hi, I'm glad you're here.
Police officer: We saw someone run out of your house.
Alfredo: Good. You scared him away.
Police officer: Is anything missing?
Alfredo: No, just the lamp is broken.
Police officer: How did he get in?
Alfredo: He came in through the window.
Police officer: Okay, lock all your windows and doors.
Alfredo: I will. Can you drive by again later?
Police officer: Sure, we'll check around here again in an hour.

PAIR/GROUP WORK
Ask your partner or group the following questions.

1. Do you lock all your doors and windows at night? Why?
2. Do you leave any lights on at night? Why?
3. Do you have a watchdog? Why? Why not?
4. Is your neighborhood safe? Why? Why not?
5. You hear someone breaking into your house. What do you do?
6. What is neighborhood watch?
7. Your neighbors are away. Do you watch their house?

Noisy Neighbor

Look at the illustrations. Listen carefully to your teacher.

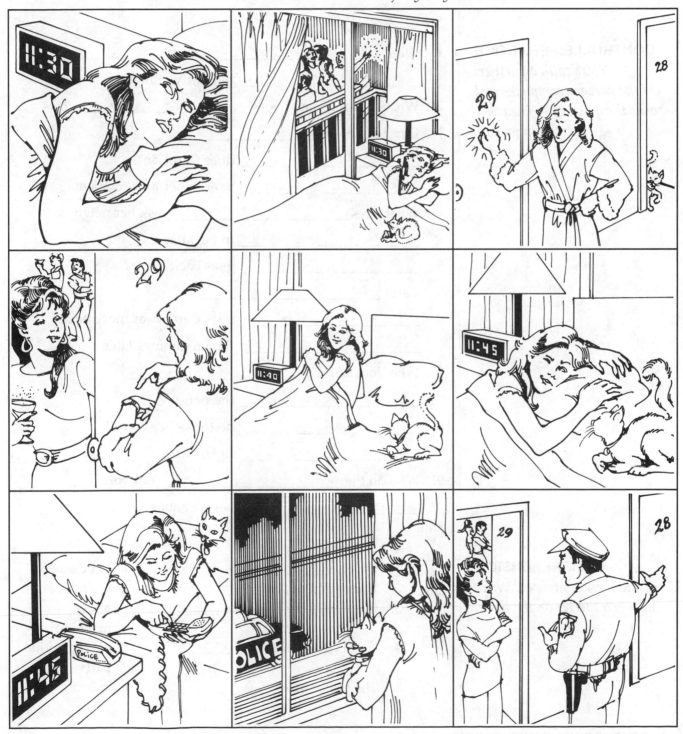

1. It's ten thirty at night.
2. Carol's neighbor is having a loud party.
3. Carol walks over to her neighbor's apartment.
4. Carol asks her neighbor to be quiet.
5. Carol goes back home and gets in bed.
6. Fifteen minutes later, she hears more noise.
7. Carol picks up the telephone and calls the police.
8. The police come to her apartment building.
9. The police talk to her neighbor.

CONTROLLED PRACTICE
*Work with a partner.
One partner completes and
asks the questions. The other
partner answers.*

1. What _____ is it?
_____ ten thirty at night.
2. What is Carol's neighbor _____ ?
Her neighbor is _____ .
3. _____ does Carol do?
_____ over to her neighbor's house.
4. What does _____ ask her neighbor?
_____ to be quiet.
5. _____ goes back home?
Carol _____ .
6. _____ does Carol hear more noise?
_____ fifteen minutes later.
7. Who does Carol _____ ?
_____ the police.
8. _____ do the police come?
_____ right away.
9. Who do the _____ talk to?
_____ her neighbor.

COMPREHENSION
*Complete these sentences. Write
the correct letter on the lines.*

__e__ 1. Carol is _____ .
____ 2. Her neighbor is _____ .
____ 3. Carol asks her neighbor _____ .
____ 4. Carol telephones _____ .
____ 5. The police talk _____ .

a. to be quiet
b. the police
c. to her neighbor
d. having a loud party
e. in bed

DESCRIPTIVE PHASE

Answer the following questions.

1. Do you think Carol is happy or angry? Why?
2. Why does Carol go over to her neighbor's apartment?
3. What does Carol ask her neighbor?
4. Why does Carol call the police?
5. What do the police do?

ROLE PLAY

Work with a partner. You play one role. Your partner plays the other role. Then, switch roles.

Carol: Hi, I'm Carol from next door.
Neighbor: Hi, come on in. We're having a party.
Carol: No thanks. I just want to ask you a favor.
Neighbor: Sure. What's on your mind?
Carol: I have to work early in the morning.
Neighbor: Yeah, so?
Carol: Could you turn down the music some?
Neighbor: Sure, no problem.
Carol: Thanks, I really am tired.
Neighbor: Good night. I'm sorry we bothered you.

PAIR/GROUP WORK

Ask your partner or group the following questions.

1. Do you live in a house or an apartment?
2. Your neighbor asks you to turn down the stereo. What do you do?
3. Your neighbor calls the police. Do you get angry? Why? Why not?
4. Your neighbor has many loud parties. What do you do?
5. Do you have loud parties at your house?
6. What time do you usually go to bed?

Speeding

Look at the illustrations. Listen carefully to your teacher.

1. Jaime is going 45 miles per hour.
2. The speed limit is only 25 miles per hour.
3. A police officer turns on his lights and siren.
4. Jaime pulls over to the side of the road.
5. The police officer walks up to Jaime's car.
6. Jaime gives the police officer his driver's license and car registration.
7. The police officer takes out his ticket book.
8. He writes a speeding ticket.
9. Jaime signs the ticket.

CONTROLLED PRACTICE

Work with a partner. One partner completes and asks the questions. The other partner answers.

1. How _____ is Jaime going in his sports car?

   _____ 45 miles per hour.

2. What is the _____ limit?

   _____ only 25 miles per hour.

3. _____ does the police officer do?

   _____ turns on his lights and siren.

4. _____ pulls over to the side of the road?

   Jaime _____ .

5. What _____ the police officer do then?

   _____ walks up to Jaime's car.

6. What does Jaime _____ the police officer?

   _____ his driver's license and car registration.

7. What does the police officer _____ out?

   _____ his ticket book.

8. _____ does the police officer write?

   _____ a speeding ticket.

9. What does _____ sign?

   _____ the ticket.

COMPREHENSION

Read the sentences. Then, write true, false, or maybe on the lines.

_____ 1. Jaime is driving too slow.

_____ 2. Jaime is driving above the speed limit.

_____ 3. The police officer is angry.

_____ 4. The police officer looks at Jaime's license.

_____ 5. Jaime is afraid.

_____ 6. Jaime gets a speeding ticket.

DESCRIPTIVE PHASE

Answer the following questions.

1. How fast is Jaime going?
2. What is the speed limit?
3. What does Jaime give the police officer?
4. What does the police officer take out?
5. Who signs the ticket?

ROLE PLAY

Work with a partner. You play one role. Your partner plays the other role. Then, switch roles.

Police officer: Could I see your license, sir?
Jaime: Sure, here it is.
Police officer: You're Jaime Rivera?
Jaime: Yes, I am.
Police officer: Is this your car, Jaime?
Jaime: Yes, it is.
Police officer: Do you know what the speed limit is?
Jaime: Not really. I didn't see any signs.
Police officer: It's only 25 miles per hour.
Jaime: I guess you're going to give me a ticket.
Police officer: Yes, I am.

PAIR/GROUP WORK

Ask your partner or group the following questions.

1. Do you drive a car? Why? Why not?
2. Do you drive fast or slow?
3. An officer turns on his flashing lights behind your car. What do you do?
4. What's the speed limit on your street?
5. What's the speed limit in school zones?
6. What's the speed limit on the freeway?

Take Care of Yourself

At the Dentist

Look at the illustrations. Listen carefully to your teacher.

13

1. Maria is at the dentist's office.
2. She has a bad toothache.
3. She signs in at the receptionist's desk.
4. The receptionist gives her a medical history form.
5. She writes down her name, address, and phone number.
6. She checks off the answers to medical questions.
7. She signs the form at the bottom.
8. She gives the form back to the receptionist.
9. The receptionist takes her to the examination room.

CONTROLLED PRACTICE
*Work with a partner.
One partner completes and
asks the questions. The other
partner answers.*

1. _____ is Maria?

   _____ at the dentist's office.

2. _____ the problem?

   _____ a bad toothache.

3. Where does she _____ in?

   _____ at the receptionist's desk.

4. What does the _____ give her?

   _____ a medical history form.

5. What does she _____ down?

   _____ her name, address, and phone

   number.

6. What does she _____ off?

   _____ the answers to medical questions.

7. _____ does she sign the form?

   _____ at the bottom.

8. Who does she _____ the form back to?

   _____ the receptionist.

9. Where does the receptionist _____ her?

   _____ the examination room.

COMPREHENSION

Complete these sentences. Write the correct letter on the lines.

__e__ 1. Maria has _____ .

_____ 2. Maria signs in at the _____ .

_____ 3. Maria fills out _____ .

_____ 4. Maria checks off _____ .

_____ 5. The receptionist takes her to _____ .

a. a medical history form

b. the examination room

c. receptionist's desk

d. answers to medical questions

e. a bad toothache

DESCRIPTIVE PHASE

Answer the following questions.

1. What's wrong with Maria?
2. Where is Maria?
3. What does she fill out?
4. Where does she sign the form?
5. Where does she write her name, address, and phone number?

ROLE PLAY

Work with a partner. You play one role. Your partner plays the other role. Then, switch roles.

Receptionist: Hi, can I help you?
Maria: Yes, I have a 10:30 appointment.
Receptionist: Have you been here before?
Maria: No, I'm a new patient.
Receptionist: Okay, fill out this medical history form, please.
Maria: Okay. Here, I'm finished.
Receptionist: Maria, do you have dental insurance?
Maria: No, I sure don't.
Receptionist: Well, follow me. Have a seat. The dentist will be right in.
Maria: Thank you.

PAIR/GROUP WORK

Ask your partner or group the following questions.

1. How often do you go to the dentist?
2. What's your dentist's name?
3. Where's your dentist's office?
4. Do you have dental insurance?
5. What's the name of your dental insurance company?

A Burn

Look at the illustrations. Listen carefully to your teacher.

1. Marcos is in the kitchen cooking dinner.
2. His son touches the hot pot on the stove.
3. He jerks his hand away and yells.
4. Marcos turns on the cold water.
5. Marcos sticks his son's hand under the water.
6. Marcos gets some burn ointment out of the medicine cabinet.
7. He squeezes some ointment onto his son's hand.
8. He rubs the ointment in gently.
9. He puts a bag of ice on his son's hand.

CONTROLLED PRACTICE

Work with a partner. One partner completes and asks the questions. The other partner answers.

1. _____ is cooking dinner?

   Marcos _____ .

2. What _____ his son touch?

   _____ the hot pot.

3. What does his son _____ ?

   _____ jerks his hand away and yells.

4. What does Marcos _____ first?

   _____ turns on the cold water.

5. _____ does Marcos do next?

   _____ sticks his son's hand under cold

   water.

6. What does Marcos _____ out of the

   medicine cabinet?

   _____ some burn ointment.

7. Where does he _____ it?

   _____ onto his son's hand.

8. _____ does he rub the ointment in?

   _____ gently.

9. What else does he _____ on his son's

   hand?

   _____ a bag of ice on his son's hand.

COMPREHENSION
Read the sentences.
Then, write true, false, or
maybe on the lines.

_____ 1. Marcos is a good cook.

_____ 2. Marcos has an accident.

_____ 3. Marcos yells when his son touches the pot.

_____ 4. Marcos thinks ice is good for burns.

_____ 5. The ointment is in a tube.

DESCRIPTIVE PHASE
Answer the following questions.

1. What is Marcos doing in the kitchen?
2. What happens to Marcos's son?
3. What does Marcos do first?
4. What does Marcos do with the burn ointment?
5. What does Marcos do with the bag of ice?

ROLE PLAY
Work with a partner. You play
one role. Your partner plays the
other role. Then, switch roles.

Son: Ow! Daddy!
Marcos: What happened?
Son: I burned my hand.
Marcos: Come over to the sink. We'll put some cold water on it.
Son: Ow! It still hurts.
Marcos: Stay here. I'll get some burn ointment.
Son: That feels better. Thanks, Dad.
Marcos: Hold on, I'll get an ice bag to put on it.
Son: No, that's okay. It feels better now.

PAIR/GROUP WORK
Ask your partner or group the
following questions.

1. Do you ever burn yourself?
2. What do you put on a burn?
3. Where do you usually burn yourself?
4. Where is your medicine cabinet?
5. When do you cook?

Cough and Fever

Look at the illustrations. Listen carefully to your teacher.

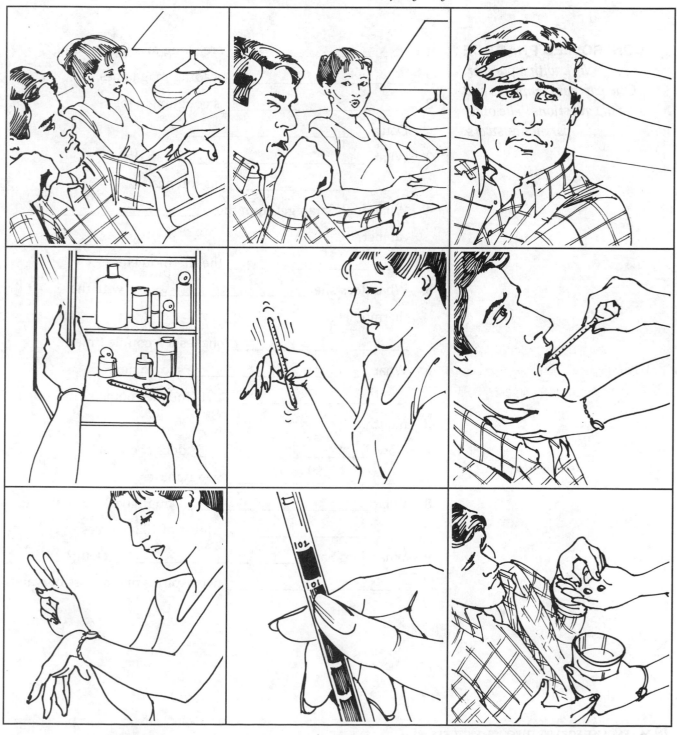

19

1. Doug and Sarah are reading magazines.
2. Doug is coughing a lot and he has a headache.
3. Sarah feels his forehead. It feels warm.
4. She gets the thermometer out of the medicine cabinet.
5. She shakes it a couple times.
6. She puts the thermometer in his mouth.
7. She waits two minutes and takes it out.
8. He has a fever of 102 degrees.
9. She gives him two aspirins and a glass of water.

CONTROLLED PRACTICE
*Work with a partner.
One partner completes and
asks the questions. The other
partner answers.*

1. _____ are Doug and Sarah doing?

   _____ reading magazines.

2. _____ is coughing a lot?

   Doug _____ .

3. What _____ Sarah do?

   _____ his forehead.

4. What does Sarah get from the _____
   cabinet?

   _____ the thermometer.

5. What does she _____ with the
   thermometer?

   _____ shakes it a couple times.

6. What _____ she do next?

   _____ puts the thermometer in Doug's
   mouth.

7. How _____ does she wait?

   _____ two minutes.

8. What _____ Doug have?

   _____ a fever of 102 degrees.

9. What does Sarah _____ Doug?

   _____ two aspirins and a glass of water.

COMPREHENSION

Complete the second line of these dialogues.

1. Doug: I'm coughing a lot.

   Sarah: *Maybe you have a cold.*

2. Doug: My forehead feels warm.

   Sarah: _____

3. Sarah: The thermometer is not working.

   Doug: _____

DESCRIPTIVE PHASE

Answer the following questions.

1. What is wrong with Doug?
2. What does Sarah do first?
3. What is Doug's temperature?
4. What does Sarah do with the thermometer?
5. What does Sarah give Doug for his fever?

ROLE PLAY

Work with a partner. You play one role. Your partner plays the other role. Then, switch roles.

Sarah: You sure are coughing a lot.
Doug: Don't worry, I'm okay.
Sarah: Your forehead feels hot.
Doug: It's nothing. Don't worry.
Sarah: I think I should take your temperature.
Doug: Okay, but it's probably normal.
Sarah: Wow! You have a fever of 102 degrees.
Doug: Oh well, I guess I'll go to bed.
Sarah: Wait a minute. I'll get you some aspirin.

PAIR/GROUP WORK

Ask your partner or group the following questions.

1. Do you cough a lot? Why?
2. What's your doctor's name?
3. What's your doctor's address?
4. How far do you live from a hospital?
5. Do you have a thermometer? Where do you keep it?
6. What kind of medicine do you take for a cough?

Twisted Ankle

Look at the illustrations. Listen carefully to your teacher.

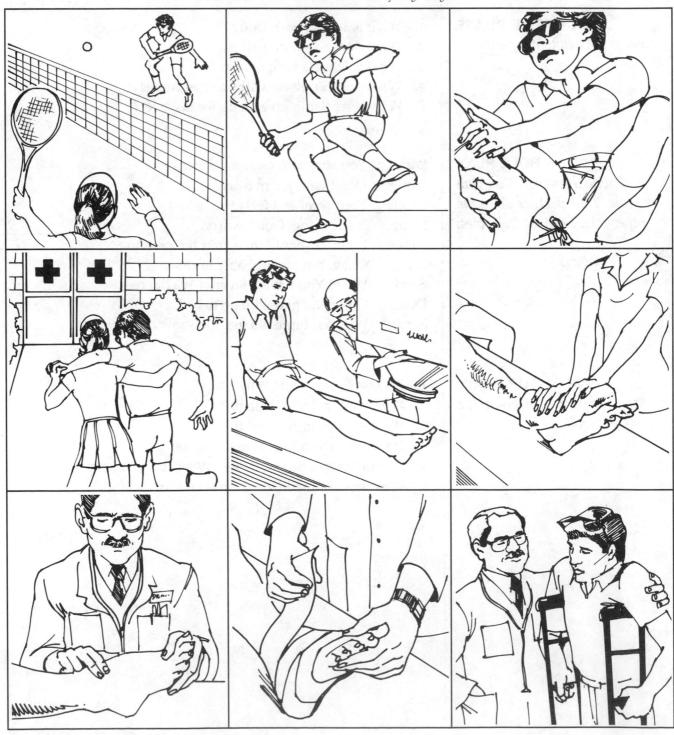

PRESENTATION
Read the following sentences.

1. Sergio and his sister are playing tennis.
2. Sergio twists his ankle and yells.
3. His ankle swells.
4. His sister takes him to the hospital.
5. The technician takes an X-ray of his ankle.
6. The nurse puts a bag of ice on his ankle.
7. The doctor examines his ankle.
8. The doctor wraps his ankle with a bandage.
9. The doctor gives Sergio some crutches.

CONTROLLED PRACTICE
*Work with a partner.
One partner completes and
asks the questions. The other
partner answers.*

1. What _____ and his sister playing?
   _____ tennis.

2. Who _____ his ankle and yells?
   Sergio _____ .

3. _____ swells?
   Sergio's ankle _____ .

4. _____ does his sister take him?
   _____ to the hospital.

5. What _____ the technician do?
   _____ takes an X-ray of Sergio's ankle.

6. What does the nurse _____ on his
   ankle?
   _____ a bag of ice
   _____ .

7. _____ examines his ankle?
   The doctor _____ .

8. What does the doctor _____ ?
   _____ his ankle.

9. What does the doctor _____ Sergio?
   _____ some crutches.

COMPREHENSION

Contradict these sentences.

1. Sergio is playing basketball.

   No, he isn't.

2. Sergio doesn't twist his ankle.

   _____

3. Sergio's sister takes him to the clinic.

   _____

4. The doctor takes an X-ray of Sergio's ankle.

   _____

5. The nurse wraps his ankle with a bandage.

   _____

6. The nurse gives Sergio crutches.

   _____

DESCRIPTIVE PHASE

Answer the following questions.

1. Why does Sergio yell?
2. Who takes Sergio to the hospital?
3. Who puts ice on Sergio's ankle?
4. What does the doctor do first?
5. What does the doctor give Sergio?

ROLE PLAY

Work with a partner. You play one role. Your partner plays the other role. Then, switch roles.

Doctor: Tell me what happened.
Sergio: I twisted my ankle playing tennis.
Doctor: You're lucky. It's not broken.
Sergio: Are you sure? It really hurts.
Doctor: Yes, it's just a bad sprain.
Sergio: Can I walk on it?
Doctor: No. I want you to use crutches for a week.
Sergio: Anything else?
Doctor: Keep putting ice on it until the swelling goes down.

PAIR/GROUP WORK

Ask your partner or group the following questions.

1. What sports do you play?
2. You twist your ankle playing soccer. What do you do?
3. Your ankle is swollen. What do you do?
4. Do you want to be an X-ray technician?
5. Are you wearing a cast? Why? Why not?

You Are What You Eat

Sugar and Salt

Look at the illustrations. Listen carefully to your teacher.

PRESENTATION
Read the following sentences.

1. Ms. Baker and her son are shopping for cereal.
2. Her son picks out a box of cereal.
3. Ms. Baker reads the ingredients on the side of the box.
4. The cereal contains lots of sugar and salt.
5. She tells her son to put it back.
6. She picks out another cereal.
7. She looks at the label.
8. It says, "no sugar" and "no salt."
9. She puts it in her cart.

CONTROLLED PRACTICE
Work with a partner. One partner completes and asks the questions. The other partner answers.

1. What _____ Ms. Baker and her son shopping for?

_____ cereal.

2. What does her son _____ out?

_____ a box of cereal.

3. What does Ms. Baker _____ on the side of the box?

_____ the ingredients.

4. What does the _____ contain?

_____ lots of sugar and salt.

5. What does Ms. Baker tell her son to _____?

_____ to put it back.

6. What _____ Ms. Baker do next?

_____ picks out another cereal.

7. What _____ she look at?

_____ at the label.

8. _____ does it say?

_____ , "No sugar and no salt."

9. Where does she _____ it?

_____ in her cart.

COMPREHENSION

Complete these sentences. Write the correct letter on the lines.

__d__ 1. Ms. Baker tells her son _____.

_____ 2. Her son picks out _____.

_____ 3. Ms. Baker _____.

_____ 4. The first box of cereal has _____.

_____ 5. The second box of cereal has _____.

a. reads the ingredients on the box

b. lots of sugar and salt

c. a box of cereal

d. to put the cereal back

e. no sugar and no salt

DESCRIPTIVE PHASE

Answer the following questions.

1. Who is shopping with Ms. Baker?
2. What does Ms. Baker tell her son?
3. What does the first box of cereal contain?
4. Why does Ms. Baker tell her son to put the cereal back?
5. Who reads the label on the box?

ROLE PLAY

Work with a partner. You play one role. Your partner plays the other role. Then, switch roles.

Son:	Momma, Momma, I want this kind of cereal.
Ms. Baker:	Let me see it.
Son:	It's really good, just like candy.
Ms. Baker:	Put it back. It has too much sugar and salt.
Son:	Ah, Mom, come on, please.
Ms. Baker:	Don't argue. We'll get this one.
Son:	Yuck! That stuff's terrible.
Ms. Baker:	But it's good for you.
Son:	Okay, but I don't like it.

PAIR/GROUP WORK

Ask your partner or group the following questions.

1. What do you eat for breakfast?
2. Do you eat hot or cold cereal for breakfast?
3. What do you put on your cereal?
4. What is your favorite cereal?
5. Do you read the labels on boxes of food? Why? Why not?

Getting a Rain Check

Look at the illustrations. Listen carefully to your teacher.

1. Monica is reading the newspaper.
2. She sees an ad for margarine.
3. It's on sale for half-price.
4. She goes to the market to buy a couple pounds of margarine.
5. The market is out of margarine.
6. She shows the ad to the cashier.
7. The cashier gives her a rain check for two pounds of margarine.
8. The rain check says, "Out of stock — Can purchase next week at sale price."
9. Monica buys margarine for half-price a week later.

CONTROLLED PRACTICE

Work with a partner. One partner completes and asks the questions. The other partner answers.

1. _____ is Monica reading?

   _____ the newspaper.

2. What does _____ see?

   _____ an ad for margarine.

3. How _____ is it on sale for?

   _____ half-price.

4. Why does she _____ to the market?

   _____ a couple pounds of margarine.

5. _____ is the market out of?

   _____ margarine.

6. What does she _____ with the ad?

   _____ shows the ad to the cashier.

7. What does the cashier _____ her?

   _____ a rain check.

8. _____ can she buy more margarine?

   _____ next week.

9. How much _____ Monica buy the margarine for a week later?

   _____ half-price.

COMPREHENSION
Contradict the following sentences.

1. Monica is watching TV.
   No, she isn't.

2. Monica wants to buy some dog food.

   _____

3. The margarine is regular price.

   _____

4. The market has a lot of margarine.

   _____

5. The cashier does not give her anything.

   _____

6. Monica can't purchase margarine a week later.

   _____

DESCRIPTIVE PHASE
Answer the following questions.

1. What is Monica doing?
2. Where does she see the ad for margarine?
3. Is the margarine on sale? For how much?
4. What does she show to the cashier?
5. When can she buy the margarine?

ROLE PLAY
Work with a partner. You play one role. Your partner plays the other role. Then, switch roles.

Monica:	Excuse me, the margarine shelf is empty.
Cashier:	I'm sorry, we must be all out.
Monica:	When will you get more in?
Cashier:	Not until next week.
Monica:	But the sale ends tomorrow.
Cashier:	That's okay. I can give you a rain check.
Monica:	What's a rain check?
Cashier:	A note or a ticket that lets you buy an item later at the sale price.
Monica:	So, I can buy the margarine for the sale price next week?
Cashier:	You sure can.

PAIR/GROUP WORK
Ask your partner or group the following questions.

1. Where can you find ads for sales?
2. Does your market give rain checks?
3. How often do you use coupons?
4. Do you buy clothes or groceries with coupons?

Paying with a Check

Look at the illustrations. Listen carefully to your teacher.

1. Ms. Douglas brings her shopping cart to the checkout lane.
2. The cashier rings up her groceries.
3. Ms. Douglas takes out her checkbook.
4. She writes a check for the total.
5. Ms. Douglas shows her driver's license and a credit card to the cashier.
6. The cashier writes the driver's license and credit card numbers on the check.
7. The bagger asks Ms. Douglas if she wants paper or plastic bags.
8. Ms. Douglas says, "Paper, please."
9. The bagger bags her groceries and puts them in her cart.

CONTROLLED PRACTICE
*Work with a partner.
One partner completes and
asks the questions. The other
partner answers.*

1. Where does Ms. Douglas take her _____?
   _____ to the checkout lane.

2. Who rings up her _____ ?
   The cashier _____ .

3. What does Ms. Douglas _____ out?
   _____ her checkbook.

4. What does _____ write a check for?
   _____ the total.

5. What does Ms. Douglas _____ to the cashier?
   _____ her driver's license and a credit card.

6. What does the cashier write on the _____?
   _____ the driver's license and credit card numbers.

7. _____ does the bagger ask Ms. Douglas?
   _____ if she wants paper or plastic.

8. _____ Ms. Douglas say?
   _____ "Paper, please."

9. Who _____ all her groceries and puts them in the cart?
   The bagger _____ .

COMPREHENSION

Complete the second line of these dialogues.

1. Ms. Douglas: I don't have any cash.

   Cashier: *You can write a check.*

2. Bag person: Do you want paper or plastic?

   Ms. Douglas: _____

3. Cashier: May I see your driver's license and a credit card, please.

   Ms. Douglas: _____

DESCRIPTIVE PHASE

Answer the following questions.

1. Where does Ms. Douglas bring her shopping cart?
2. What is in the cart?
3. How does Ms. Douglas pay for her groceries?
4. What does Ms. Douglas show the cashier?
5. What does the cashier write on the check?
6. What kind of bags does Ms. Douglas want?

ROLE PLAY

Work with a partner. You play one role. Your partner plays the other role. Then, switch roles.

Cashier: Good afternoon. How are you?
Ms. Douglas: Fine, thanks.
Cashier: Will this be cash or check?
Ms. Douglas: Check. What's the total?
Cashier: It comes to $53.89.
Ms. Douglas: Okay, here's my check.
Cashier: Thanks. I need to see your driver's license and a credit card.
Ms. Douglas: Okay, here you are.
Cashier: Okay, let's see . . . N38456217. Thanks.
Ms. Douglas: You're welcome.

PAIR/GROUP WORK

Ask your partner or group the following questions.

1. Where do you go shopping?
2. How do you pay for your groceries?
3. Does your market take checks?
4. What kind of ID do you have?
5. Do you have a credit card?
6. Do you prefer paper or plastic bags?

Expiration Date

Look at the illustrations. Listen carefully to your teacher.

PRESENTATION

Read the following sentences.

1. Mr. Baker goes to the corner market to buy milk for his children.
2. He picks up a half-gallon of milk.
3. He checks the expiration date.
4. He picks up another carton.
5. He takes them up to the cashier.
6. The cashier rings them up.
7. Mr. Baker gives the cashier a five-dollar bill.
8. The cashier gives him his change and receipt.
9. He puts his change and receipt in his pocket.

CONTROLLED PRACTICE

*Work with a partner.
One partner completes and
asks the questions. The other
partner answers.*

1. Where does Mr. Baker _____ ?

    _____ to the corner market.

2. What does he _____ up?

    _____ a half-gallon of milk.

3. _____ does he check?

    _____ the expiration date.

4. _____ does he pick up next?

    _____ another carton.

5. Where does he _____ them?

    _____ up to the cashier.

6. _____ rings them up?

    The cashier _____ .

7. What _____ Mr. Baker give the cashier?

    _____ a five-dollar bill.

8. What does the _____ give him?

    _____ his change and receipt.

9. What does he put in his _____ ?

    _____ in his pocket.

COMPREHENSION

Read the sentences.
Then, write true, false, or
maybe on the lines.

_____ 1. There is a corner market near Mr. Baker's house.

_____ 2. Mr. Baker buys only one carton of milk.

_____ 3. He is careful about the food he buys.

_____ 4. Mr. Baker pays cash for the milk.

_____ 5. Mr. Baker's children like milk.

_____ 6. The cashier puts a receipt in Mr. Baker's pocket.

DESCRIPTIVE PHASE

Answer the following questions.

1. Where does Mr. Baker shop for milk?
2. How much milk does he buy?
3. Does he pay more or less than five dollars?
4. Does Mr. Baker pay with a check or cash?
5. What does he get from the cashier?

ROLE PLAY

Work with a partner. You play
one role. Your partner plays the
other role. Then, switch roles.

Mr. Baker: Excuse me. Where's the expiration date on this?
Cashier: It's on the top of the carton.
Mr. Baker: Oh, there it is. It expires the sixteenth.
Cashier: Yes, and today is only the tenth.
Mr. Baker: Wow! Your milk sure is fresh.
Cashier: Your total is $3.22.
Mr. Baker: Out of five dollars.
Cashier: And here's your change.

PAIR/GROUP WORK

Ask your partner or group the
following questions.

1. Where do you buy your milk?
2. How much milk do you buy a week?
3. How much do you pay for a gallon of milk?
4. Where is the expiration date on your milk?
5. What do you do if you buy bad milk?
6. What kind of milk do you buy?
7. Do you like chocolate milk?

If It Fits, Wear It

Shoes for Everyone

Look at the illustrations. Listen carefully to your teacher.

1. Mr. Ochoa wants to buy tennis shoes for his two daughters.
2. The salesclerk measures their feet.
3. He goes into the back room to get their shoes.
4. They try on the new shoes.
5. They walk around the store.
6. Mr. Ochoa says, "I'll take them."
7. The girls put their old shoes in the boxes.
8. Mr. Ochoa pays for the shoes with his credit card.
9. He signs the slip and writes down his phone number.

CONTROLLED PRACTICE
Work with a partner. One partner completes and asks the questions. The other partner answers.

1. What does Mr. Ochoa _____ to buy for his two daughters?

   _____ tennis shoes.

2. Who _____ their feet?

   The salesclerk _____ .

3. _____ does he go to get their shoes?

   _____ into the back room.

4. What _____ they try on?

   _____ the new shoes.

5. _____ do they walk?

   _____ around the store.

6. What does Mr. Ochoa _____ ?

   _____ , "I'll take them."

7. Where do they _____ their old shoes?

   _____ in the boxes.

8. How does Mr. Ochoa _____ for the shoes?

   _____ with his credit card.

9. What does he _____ ?

   _____ the slip.

COMPREHENSION

COMPREHENSION
Complete the second line of these dialogues.

1. Salesclerk: How may I help you?
   Mr. Ochoa: *I need some tennis shoes.*

2. Salesclerk: What size do you wear?
   Mr. Ochoa: _____

3. Salesclerk: Will this be cash or charge?
   Mr. Ochoa: _____

DESCRIPTIVE PHASE
Answer the following questions.

1. What kind of shoes does Mr. Ochoa want to buy for his daughters?
2. Where does the salesclerk go to get their shoes?
3. Does Mr. Ochoa buy the shoes?
4. Where do the girls put their old shoes?
5. How does Mr. Ochoa pay for the shoes?
6. Where does Mr. Ochoa write his phone number?

ROLE PLAY
Work with a partner. You play one role. Your partner plays the other role. Then, switch roles.

Salesclerk: Hi. May I help you?
Mr. Ochoa: Sure. I need some tennis shoes for my daughters.
Salesclerk: What color?
Mr. Ochoa: Do you have blue?
Salesclerk: Sure we do. What sizes?
Mr. Ochoa: I'm not sure.
Salesclerk: That's okay. I'll measure them.
Mr. Ochoa: Well, what do you think?
Salesclerk: She needs a 7D and she needs a 5B.

PAIR/GROUP WORK
Ask your partner or group the following questions.

1. Where do you buy your shoes?
2. What size do you wear?
3. What brand of tennis shoes do you like?
4. What color shoes do you prefer?
5. Do you wear tennis shoes?
6. How much do you pay for dress shoes?

Returning Merchandise

Look at the illustrations. Listen carefully to your teacher.

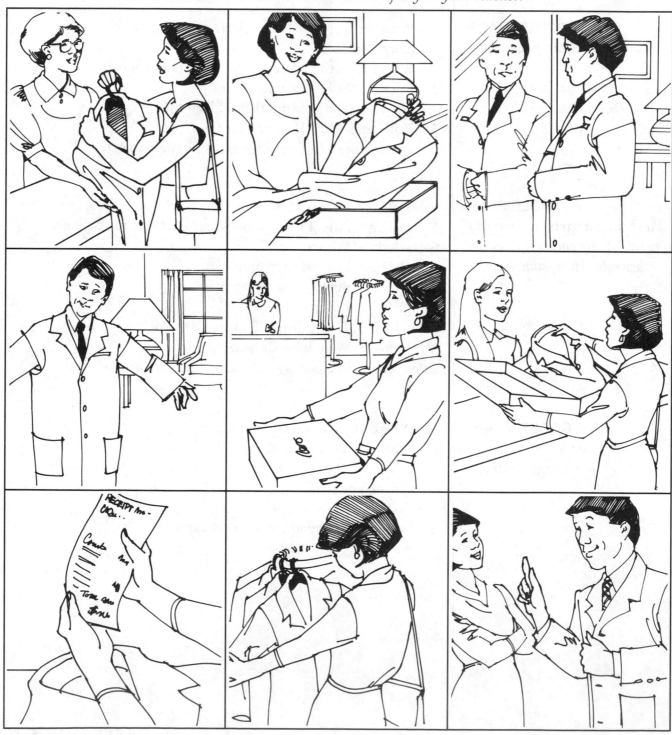

PRESENTATION

Read the following sentences.

1. Ms. Ko buys an overcoat for her husband.
2. She takes it home to her husband.
3. He puts on the overcoat and looks in the mirror.
4. It doesn't fit. It's much too big.
5. Ms. Ko takes the overcoat back to the store.
6. She returns the overcoat to the salesclerk.
7. She shows her the receipt.
8. She gets a smaller sized overcoat.
9. She takes it back home to her husband.

CONTROLLED PRACTICE

Work with a partner. One partner completes and asks the questions. The other partner answers.

1. What does Ms. Ko _____ for her husband?

   _____ an overcoat.

2. Where does she _____ it?

   _____ home to her husband.

3. _____ does he do?

   He puts it on and _____ in the mirror.

4. How does the _____ fit?

   _____ much too big.

5. _____ does Ms. Ko do?

   _____ takes the overcoat back to the store.

6. Who _____ she return the overcoat to?

   _____ the salesclerk.

7. What does she _____ the salesclerk?

   _____ the receipt.

8. What does she _____ ?

   _____ a smaller sized overcoat.

9. Where does she _____ it?

   _____ back home to her husband.

COMPREHENSION
Complete the second line of these dialogues.

1. Ms. Ko: What is the price of this overcoat?
   Salesclerk: It's $85.

2. Salesclerk: What size overcoat does your husband wear?
   Ms. Ko: _____

3. Salesclerk: Why do you want to return the overcoat?
   Ms. Ko: _____

DESCRIPTIVE PHASE
Answer the following questions.

1. Who does Ms. Ko buy an overcoat for?
2. Does the overcoat fit her husband?
3. What's wrong with the overcoat?
4. What does Ms. Ko do?
5. Who does Ms. Ko show the receipt to?
6. Does Ms. Ko get a refund or an exchange?

ROLE PLAY
Work with a partner. You play one role. Your partner plays the other role. Then, switch roles.

Ms. Ko: Hi, remember me?
Salesclerk: Sure, you just bought an overcoat.
Ms. Ko: Yes, but it's too big for my husband.
Salesclerk: Do you want a refund?
Ms. Ko: No, I want to exchange it.
Salesclerk: Do you have the receipt?
Ms. Ko: Sure, right here.
Salesclerk: Okay, leave that overcoat here and pick out another one.
Ms. Ko: This one looks like the right size.
Salesclerk: Good. I'll put it in a bag for you.

PAIR/GROUP WORK
Ask your partner or group the following questions.

1. Do you exchange clothing?
2. Do you save your receipts or do you throw them away?
3. Who buys your clothes?
4. Where do you shop for clothes?
5. What size overcoat do you wear?

Make Sure Your Pants Fit

Look at the illustrations. Listen carefully to your teacher.

1. Roberto goes to the men's department to buy some pants.
2. The salesclerk measures his waist. It's 29 inches.
3. His inseam is 30 inches.
4. The salesclerk shows him a rack of pants that are his size.
5. He takes one pair of pants into the dressing room to try on.
6. He puts on the new pair and stands in front of the mirror.
7. They fit great.
8. He takes them off and puts on his old pants.
9. He pays cash for the new pair of pants.

CONTROLLED PRACTICE
*Work with a partner.
One partner completes and
asks the questions. The other
partner answers.*

1. _____ does Roberto go to the men's department?

   _____ to buy some pants.

2. What does the _____ do?

   He measures his _____ .

3. His inseam is _____ .

   _____ 29 inches.

4. Who _____ him a rack of pants?

   The salesclerk _____ .

5. What does he _____ into the dressing room?

   He takes _____ into the dressing room.

6. _____ does he stand?

   _____ in front of the mirror.

7. How do _____ fit?

   _____ great.

8. _____ does he take off?

   _____ his new pants

   _____ .

9. How does he _____ for the new pants?

   He pays _____ .

COMPREHENSION
Read the sentences.
Then, write true, false, or
maybe on the lines.

_____ 1. Roberto wants new pants.

_____ 2. Roberto knows the size of his pants.

_____ 3. The salesclerk shows him a rack of all pants in the store.

_____ 4. Roberto tries on the pants in the dressing room.

_____ 5. The pants look terrible.

_____ 6. Roberto uses his credit card to pay for the pants.

DESCRIPTIVE PHASE
Answer the following questions.

1. Who buys some new pants?
2. What does the salesclerk measure?
3. What does the salesclerk show him?
4. Where does he try on the new pants?
5. What does he do after he looks in the mirror?
6. How many pairs of pants does he buy?

ROLE PLAY
Work with a partner. You play
one role. Your partner plays the
other role. Then, switch roles.

Roberto: Hi, I need some pants.
Salesclerk: For casual or dress?
Roberto: Oh, just casual.
Salesclerk: Do you know what size you wear?
Roberto: No, not really.
Salesclerk: Here, let me measure you.
Roberto: Well, what size am I?
Salesclerk: You're a 29 waist and a 30 inch inseam.
Roberto: Thanks.
Salesclerk: You'll find your size on these two racks.
Roberto: Okay, where's the dressing room?
Salesclerk: Right over there, by the mirrors.

PAIR/GROUP WORK
Ask your partner or group the
following questions.

1. What size waist do you have?
2. What size is your inseam?
3. Do you prefer long pants or shorts?
4. What do you wear to school or work?
5. What do you wear to a special occasion?

Buying a Shirt

Look at the illustrations. Listen carefully to your teacher.

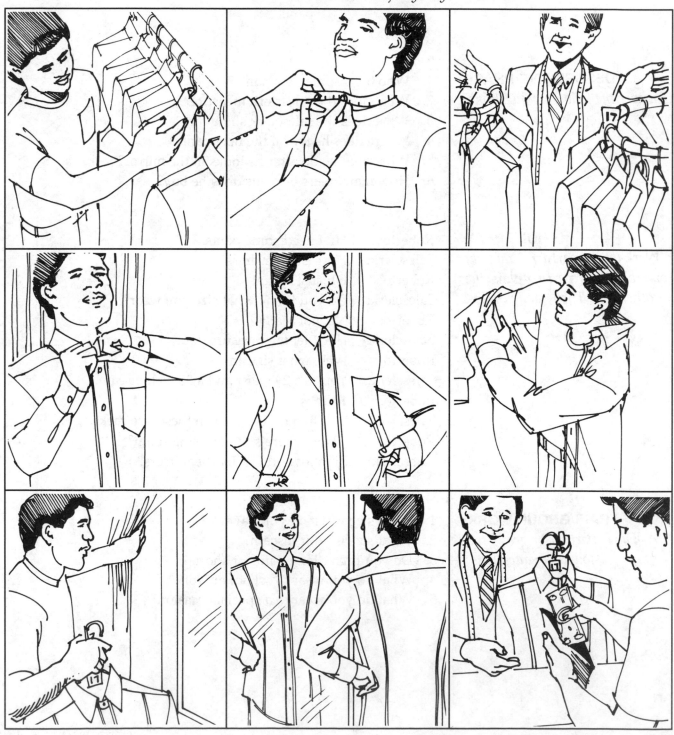

1. Mr. Warner needs to buy a new shirt.
2. The salesclerk measures his neck and it measures 17 inches.
3. The salesclerk shows him the regular-fit shirts and the tapered shirts.
4. Mr. Warner tries on a size 17 regular-fit shirt.
5. The sleeves are too long and the waist is too big.
6. He takes off the regular-fit shirt.
7. He gets a tapered shirt and goes back into the dressing room.
8. He tries on the tapered shirt and it fits.
9. He takes the shirt up to the checkstand and pays for it with cash.

CONTROLLED PRACTICE
Work with a partner. One partner completes and asks the questions. The other partner answers.

1. Who needs to _____ a new shirt?
   Mr. Warner _____ .

2. _____ the salesclerk measure?
   _____ his neck.

3. What _____ the salesclerk show him?
   _____ the regular-fit and the tapered shirts.

4. What does Mr. Warner _____ on?
   _____ a size 17 regular-fit shirt.

5. _____ is too big?
   _____ is too big.

6. What does Mr. Warner _____ off?
   _____ the regular-fit shirt.

7. _____ does he get?
   He _____ a tapered shirt.

8. _____ does he try on next?
   _____ the tapered shirt.

9. Where _____ he take the shirt?
   _____ up to the checkstand.

COMPREHENSION
Contradict the following sentences.

1. The salesclerk measures Mr. Warner's shoulders.
   No, he doesn't.

2. Mr. Warner has a 17-1/2 inch neck.

3. The salesclerk sells Mr. Warner two kinds of shirts.

4. First, Mr. Warner tries on a tapered shirt.

5. The salesclerk doesn't measure Mr. Warner's neck.

6. Mr. Warner doesn't buy the shirt.

DESCRIPTIVE PHASE
Answer the following questions.

1. Where does Mr. Warner see the shirt?
2. What size neck does Mr. Warner have?
3. What kind of shirts does the salesclerk show him?
4. Which shirt is too big for Mr. Warner?
5. Why does Mr. Warner take off the regular-fit shirt?

ROLE PLAY
Work with a partner. You play one role. Your partner plays the other role. Then, switch roles.

Salesclerk: May I help you find something?
Mr. Warner: Yes, I need a dress shirt.
Salesclerk: What size do you wear?
Mr. Warner: A sixteen or seventeen. I'm not sure.
Salesclerk: Well, I'll measure you and we'll know for sure.
Mr. Warner: What size am I?
Salesclerk: You're a seventeen. Do you want a regular-fit or tapered shirt?
Mr. Warner: I'll try the regular fit.
Salesclerk: That's a little too big around your waist.
Mr. Warner: I think so too.
Salesclerk: Why don't you try on this tapered shirt?

PAIR/GROUP WORK
Ask your partner or group the following questions.

1. What size is your neck?
2. Do you wear shirts with long sleeves or short sleeves.
3. What's your favorite color for shirts?
4. How much do you usually pay for one shirt?
5. Where do you usually buy your shirts?

Do You Have Wheels?

Overheating

Look at the illustrations. Listen carefully to your teacher.

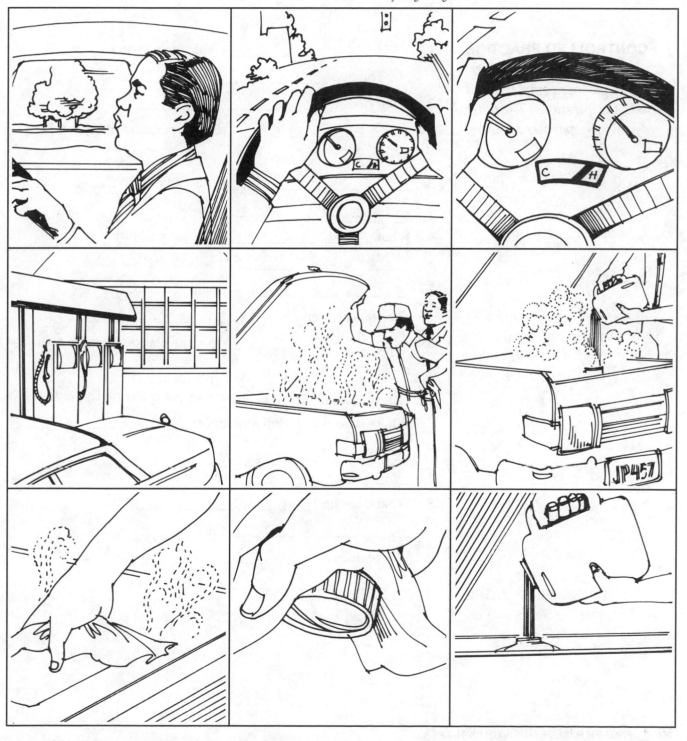

PRESENTATION
Read the following sentences.

1. Mr. Tomayo is driving to work.
2. He looks at the temperature gauge on the dashboard.
3. His car is running very hot.
4. He pulls into a service station.
5. The station attendant opens the hood.
6. The station attendant puts cold water on the radiator.
7. He puts a rag on the radiator cap.
8. He unscrews the cap and takes it off.
9. He pours water into the radiator.

CONTROLLED PRACTICE
Work with a partner. One partner completes and asks the questions. The other partner answers.

1. _____ is driving to work?

   Mr. Tomayo _____ .

2. What does he _____ at?

   _____ the temperature gauge on his

   dashboard.

3. _____ is his car running?

   _____ very hot.

4. What _____ he pull into?

   _____ a service station.

5. _____ opens the hood?

   The station attendant _____ .

6. _____ does the station attendant do

   next?

   _____ puts cold water on the radiator.

7. Where does the station attendant _____

   the rag?

   _____ on the radiator cap.

8. What does he _____ ?

   _____ the cap.

9. Where does he _____ the water?

   _____ into the radiator.

COMPREHENSION

Read the sentences.
Then, write true, false, or
maybe on the lines.

_____ 1. Mr. Tomayo takes a bus to work.

_____ 2. His car is very old.

_____ 3. The temperature gauge is on the floor.

_____ 4. He takes his car to a service station.

_____ 5. Mr. Tomayo puts cold water on his radiator.

_____ 6. Mr. Tomayo takes off the radiator cap.

DESCRIPTIVE PHASE

Answer the following questions.

1. Where is Mr. Tomayo going?
2. Where is the temperature gauge?
3. Why does he pull into a service station?
4. Who helps him?
5. How does the station attendant cool off the radiator?

ROLE PLAY

Work with a partner. You play
one role. Your partner plays the
other role. Then, switch roles.

Mr. Tomayo:	Can you help me?
Station attendant:	Sure, what's wrong?
Mr. Tomayo:	My car's overheating.
Station attendant:	Okay, pull the hood release lever.
Mr. Tomayo:	There, it's open.
Station attendant:	Stand back. I'm going to take off the radiator cap.
Mr. Tomayo:	Does it need water?
Station attendant:	It sure does. It's bone dry. I'll get some for you.
Mr. Tomayo:	Great! Thanks for your help.
Station attendant:	Don't mention it.

PAIR/GROUP WORK

Ask your partner or group the
following questions.

1. Your car is overheating. What do you do?
2. Where is the dashboard?
3. Do radiators have caps?
4. Do you put coolant in your radiator? Why?
5. Do you check the water in your radiator? How often?

Changing a Flat

Look at the illustrations. Listen carefully to your teacher.

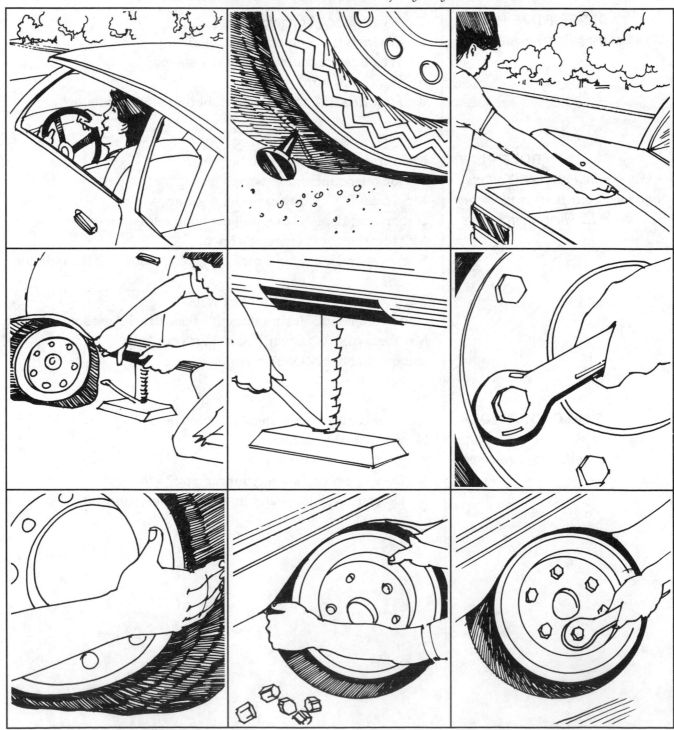

PRESENTATION
Read the following sentences.

1. Toshi and his friend are driving to the park.
2. Toshi runs over a nail and his tire goes flat.
3. He stops and opens the trunk.
4. He puts the jack under the car.
5. He jacks up the car.
6. He unscrews the lug bolts with a lug wrench.
7. He takes off the flat tire.
8. He puts on the spare tire.
9. He tightens the lug bolts.

CONTROLLED PRACTICE
Work with a partner.
One partner completes and
asks the questions. The other
partner answers.

1. Where _____ Toshi and his friend

   going?

   _____ to the park.

2. _____ does Toshi run over?

   _____ a nail.

3. What does _____ do?

   _____ the trunk.

4. _____ does he put the jack?

   _____ under the car.

5. What _____ he jack up?

   _____ the car.

6. _____ does he unscrew the lug bolts?

   _____ with a lug wrench.

7. What does he _____ off?

   _____ the flat tire.

8. What does he _____ on?

   _____ the spare tire.

9. What _____ he tighten?

   _____ the lug bolts.

COMPREHENSION

Complete these sentences. Write the correct letter on the lines.

_e__ 1. Toshi's friend _____ .

_____ 2. Toshi unscrews _____ .

_____ 3. Toshi opens _____ .

_____ 4. Toshi puts the jack under _____ .

_____ 5. Toshi takes off _____ .

_____ 6. Toshi puts on _____ .

a. the lug bolts

b. the car

c. the flat tire

d. the spare tire

e. is not driving the car

f. the trunk

DESCRIPTIVE PHASE

Answer the following questions.

1. Where are Toshi and his friend going?
2. Why do they stop?
3. Who changes the tire?
4. Where does he get the jack?
5. Toshi takes off the flat tire. What does he do before that?

ROLE PLAY

Work with a partner. You play one role. Your partner plays the other role. Then, switch roles.

Friend: Toshi, what's wrong with the car?

Toshi: I think I ran over a nail.

Friend: Oh no, we'd better stop.

Toshi: Okay, I'll pull over. Yep, it's flat.

Friend: Can you change it?

Toshi: Sure, it's easy.

Friend: Do you want me to help you?

Toshi: No, just watch out for oncoming cars.

PAIR/GROUP WORK

Ask your partner or group the following questions.

1. You get a flat tire. What do you do?
2. Where is the jack in your car?
3. Where is your spare tire?
4. How much does it cost to fix a flat tire?
5. Can you change tires?

Oil Change

Look at the illustrations. Listen carefully to your teacher.

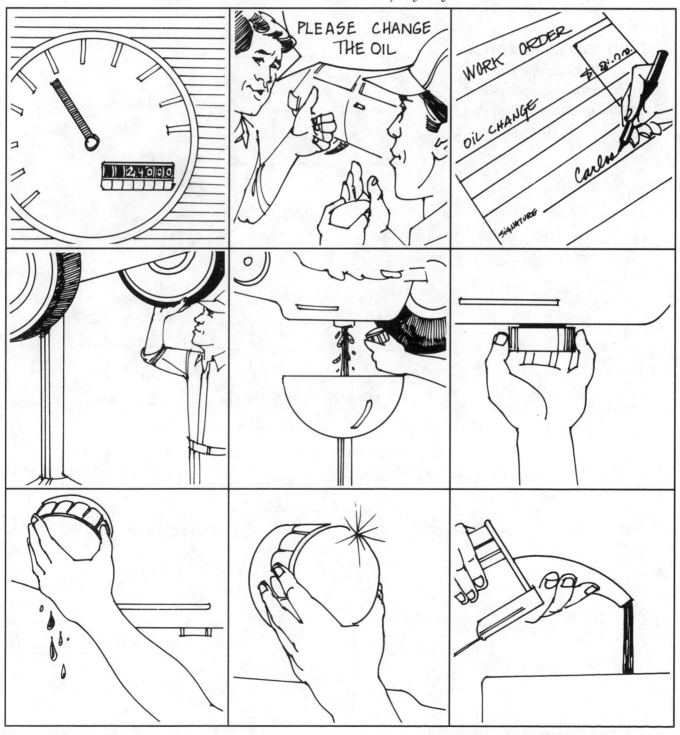

PRESENTATION

Read the following sentences.

1. Every 6,000 miles, Carlos takes his car to the mechanic.
2. He asks the mechanic to change the oil.
3. Carlos signs the work order.
4. The mechanic jacks up the car.
5. The mechanic unscrews the bolt and the oil drains out.
6. He screws the bolt back on the pan.
7. He unscrews the old oil filter.
8. He screws on the new oil filter.
9. He pours some new oil into the engine.

CONTROLLED PRACTICE

Work with a partner. One partner completes and asks the questions. The other partner answers.

1. _____ often does Carlos take his car to

   the mechanic?

   _____ every 6,000 miles.

2. What does he _____ the mechanic?

   _____ to change the oil.

3. _____ signs the work order?

   Carlos _____ .

4. What _____ the mechanic do?

   _____ the car.

5. What _____ out?

   The oil _____ .

6. _____ does he put the bolt?

   _____ back in the pan.

7. What does he do with the old _____

   filter?

   He unscrews _____ .

8. What does he _____ on?

   _____ the new oil filter.

9. _____ does he pour the oil?

   _____ into the engine.

COMPREHENSION
Read the sentences.
Then, write true, false, or
maybe on the lines.

_____ 1. There are more than 7,000 miles on Carlos' car.

_____ 2. The mechanic signs the work order.

_____ 3. Carlos paid $12.00 for the oil change.

_____ 4. The mechanic screws on the new oil filter.

_____ 5. Carlos pours new oil into the engine.

DESCRIPTIVE PHASE
Answer the following questions.

1. Where does Carlos take his car?
2. Why does Carlos take his car to the mechanic?
3. What does Carlos sign?
4. Who jacks up the car?
5. What does the mechanic put back in the pan?
6. What does he pour into the engine?

ROLE PLAY
Work with a partner. You play
one role. Your partner plays the
other role. Then, switch roles.

Carlos: Hi, could I get my oil changed?
Mechanic: Sure. Where's your car?
Carlos: Right here.
Mechanic: Okay, do you want 30 or 40 weight oil?
Carlos: 30 weight, please.
Mechanic: How about a new oil filter too?
Carlos: Why? Do I need one?
Mechanic: Yes, you do.
Carlos: How long will it take?
Mechanic: We have a few cars ahead of you. Maybe an hour or so.

PAIR/GROUP WORK
Ask your partner or group the
following questions.

1. How often do you change the oil in your car?
2. What weight oil do you use?
3. How many quarts of oil does your car take?
4. Where do you get the oil changed?
5. Who changes the oil in your car?

Alignment

Look at the illustrations. Listen carefully to your teacher.

1. Mrs. Reyes' car is shaking a lot.
2. She takes her car to a tire shop.
3. The mechanic puts her car up on a rack.
4. The front tires aren't straight.
5. The mechanic tells her she needs a front-end alignment.
6. She signs the work order.
7. She sits in the waiting room.
8. The mechanic aligns her front tires.
9. He tells her the car is ready.

CONTROLLED PRACTICE

*Work with a partner.
One partner completes and
asks the questions. The other
partner answers.*

1. _____ is the problem with Mrs. Reyes'
   car?

   _____ is shaking a lot.

2. Where does she _____ her car?

   _____ to a tire shop.

3. Where does the mechanic _____ her
   car?

   _____ up on a rack.

4. _____ tires aren't straight?

   The front tires _____ .

5. What _____ the mechanic tell her?

   _____ she needs a front-end alignment.

6. What does _____ sign?

   _____ the work order.

7. _____ does she sit?

   _____ in the waiting room.

8. What does the _____ do?

   _____ aligns her front tires.

9. What does he _____ her?

   _____ the car is ready.

COMPREHENSION
Contradict the following sentences.

1. Mrs. Reyes' car doesn't have a problem.

   Yes, it does.

2. She sells her car to a tire shop.

   _____

3. Mrs. Reyes doesn't sign the work order.

   _____

DESCRIPTIVE PHASE
Answer the following questions.

1. Why is Mrs. Reyes' car shaking?
2. Where does the mechanic put her car?
3. What does the mechanic tell her?
4. What does she sign?
5. Where does she wait?

ROLE PLAY
Work with a partner. You play one role. Your partner plays the other role. Then, switch roles.

Mechanic: Your front tires are out of alignment.
Mrs. Reyes: Oh. How much will it cost to fix them?
Mechanic: $35.
Mrs. Reyes: Can you do it today?
Mechanic: Yes. I'll start right now. I have some time.
Mrs. Reyes: Good. How long will it take?
Mechanic: About 20 minutes.
Mrs. Reyes: Where can I get a cup of coffee?
Mechanic: Over there. There's coffee in our waiting room.
Mrs. Reyes: Thank you.

PAIR/GROUP WORK
Ask your partner or group the following questions.

1. Your car is shaking a lot. What do you do?
2. Is there a tire shop near your house?
3. Who aligns your tires?
4. Do you always sign a work order?

Banking

Opening an Account

Look at the illustrations. Listen carefully to your teacher.

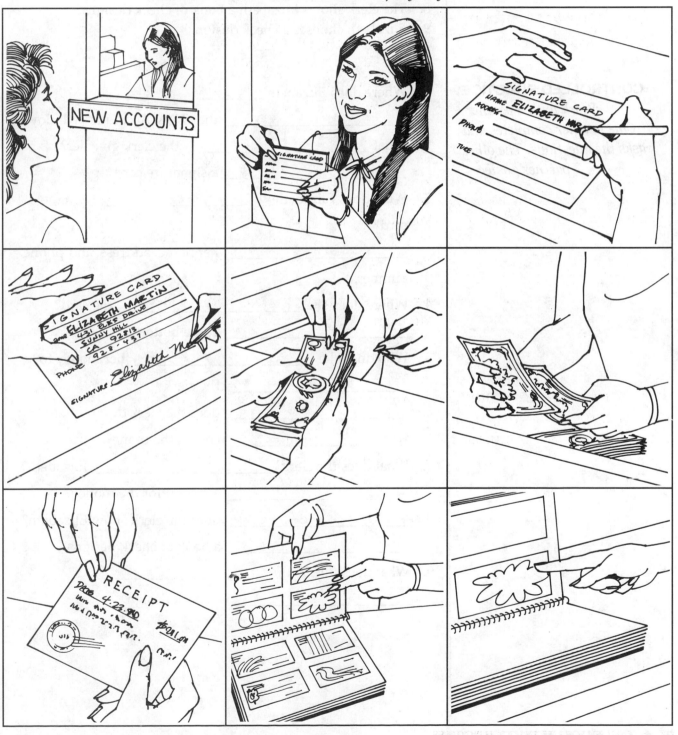

61

1. Elizabeth goes to the "New Accounts" window to open a checking account.
2. The clerk gives her a signature card.
3. Elizabeth writes her name, address, and phone number on the card.
4. Elizabeth signs the card at the bottom.
5. She gives her money to the clerk.
6. The clerk counts the money.
7. The clerk gives Elizabeth a receipt for the money.
8. The clerk shows Elizabeth a book of check designs.
9. Elizabeth chooses a check design.

CONTROLLED PRACTICE
*Work with a partner.
One partner completes and
asks the questions. The other
partner answers.*

1. Where does Elizabeth _____ ?

   _____ the "New Accounts" window.

2. What _____ the clerk give her?

   _____ a signature card.

3. What does Elizabeth _____ on the card?

   _____ her name, address, and phone number.

4. Where does she _____ the card?

   _____ at the bottom.

5. Who does she _____ her money to?

   _____ the clerk.

6. _____ does the clerk do?

   _____ counts the money.

7. What does the clerk _____ Elizabeth?

   _____ a receipt for the money.

8. _____ does the clerk show Elizabeth?

   _____ a book of check designs.

9. What does Elizabeth _____ ?

   _____ a check design.

COMPREHENSION

Read the sentences. Then, write true, false, or maybe on the lines.

_____ 1. Elizabeth has a bank account.

_____ 2. Elizabeth talks to a clerk at the "New Accounts" window.

_____ 3. Elizabeth doesn't write anything on the signature card.

_____ 4. Elizabeth picks out very pretty checks.

_____ 5. Elizabeth gets a receipt for her money.

DESCRIPTIVE PHASE

Answer the following questions.

1. Where is Elizabeth?
2. What does she want to do?
3. Who does she talk to?
4. What kind of book does Elizabeth look at?
5. What does Elizabeth choose?

ROLE PLAY

Work with a partner. You play one role. Your partner plays the other role. Then, switch roles.

Elizabeth: Hi, is this where I open an account?

Clerk: Yes, it is. I'm Sherry. I can help you.

Elizabeth: Okay, what do I do?

Clerk: First, fill out this signature card and sign it at the bottom.

Elizabeth: There, all done. Now what?

Clerk: How much do you want to deposit?

Elizabeth: Here's $200.

Clerk: Twenty, forty, sixty, eighty, one hundred, one hundred fifty, two hundred. Right. Here's your receipt.

Elizabeth: What kind of checks do I get?

Clerk: Look in this book and pick a style you like.

PAIR/GROUP WORK

Ask your partner or group the following questions.

1. What's the name of your bank?
2. What kind of account do you have?
3. How many checks do you write each month?
4. How far do you live from your bank?
5. Do you have an individual account?
6. Do you have a joint account?

Using the ATM

Look at the illustrations. Listen carefully to your teacher.

PRESENTATION
Read the following sentences.

1. The bank is closed, but Ms. Tanaka needs some money.
2. She walks up to the teller machine outside the bank.
3. She puts her bank card in the slot.
4. She punches in her secret code.
5. She pushes the "withdraw cash" button.
6. The machine asks her, "from checking or savings?"
7. She pushes the "from checking" button.
8. She punches in $100.
9. Her money comes out and she counts it.

CONTROLLED PRACTICE
Work with a partner.
One partner completes and
asks the questions. The other
partner answers.

1. What does Ms. Tanaka _____ ?
   _____ some money.
2. What _____ she do?
   She _____ to the teller machine outside the bank.
3. Where does she _____ her card?
   _____ in the slot.
4. _____ does she punch in?
   _____ her secret code.
5. _____ button does she push?
   _____ the "withdraw cash" button.
6. What does the _____ ask her?
   _____ , "from checking or savings?"
7. _____ button does she push next?
   _____ "from checking" button.
8. _____ does she punch in?
   _____ $100.
9. _____ does she count?
   _____ her money.

COMPREHENSION

Contradict the following sentences.

1. The bank is open.

   No, it's not.

2. Ms. Tanaka goes inside the bank.

3. Ms. Tanaka wants to put money in the bank.

4. Ms. Tanaka doesn't have a secret code.

5. She gets the money from her savings account.

DESCRIPTIVE PHASE

Answer the following questions.

1. Why does Ms. Tanaka go to the ATM?
2. What does she put into the slot?
3. What is the first thing she punches in?
4. What does Ms. Tanaka want to do?
5. How much money does she take out?

ROLE PLAY

Work with a partner. You play one role. Your partner plays the other role. Then, switch roles.

Ms. Tanaka: Excuse me. Could you tell me how to work this machine?

Friend: Sure, put your card in there and punch in your secret code.

Ms. Tanaka: Please, don't look.

Friend: I won't. Now, how much money do you want?

Ms. Tanaka: Just $100.

Friend: Do you want it from your checking or savings account?

Ms. Tanaka: From my checking account.

Friend: Okay, push the "from checking" button.

Ms. Tanaka: Is that it? Am I done?

Friend: No. Now punch in $100 and your money will come out.

PAIR/GROUP WORK

Ask your partner or group the following questions.

1. Do you have a bank account? Why? Why not?
2. Do you have a card for an ATM?
3. Are you afraid to use an ATM?
4. How much money can you take out of your machine?
5. How often do you use your bank's ATM?

Deposit with Cash Back

Look at the illustrations. Listen carefully to your teacher.

67

PRESENTATION

Read the following sentences.

1. Every Friday, Ms. Cruz brings her paycheck to the bank.
2. She takes out her checkbook and check register.
3. She tears out a deposit slip from her checkbook.
4. She writes the check number on the deposit slip.
5. She writes the amount of her check on the deposit slip.
6. She writes $50 in the "less cash" space.
7. She subtracts $50 and writes the balance.
8. She signs the deposit slip and the check.
9. The teller gives her $50 and a receipt for the deposit.

CONTROLLED PRACTICE

Work with a partner. One partner completes and asks the questions. The other partner answers.

1. _____ does Ms. Cruz take her paycheck?

   _____ to the bank.

2. What does she _____ first at the bank?

   _____ her checkbook and check register.

3. What does she _____ from her checkbook?

   _____ a deposit slip.

4. Where _____ she write the check number?

   _____ on the deposit slip.

5. _____ does she write on the deposit slip?

   _____ the amount of her check.

6. _____ does she write $50?

   _____ in the "less cash" space.

7. _____ much does she subtract?

   _____ $50.

8. _____ does she sign?

   _____ the deposit slip and the check.

9. _____ does the teller give Ms. Cruz?

   _____ $50 and a receipt for the deposit.

COMPREHENSION
*Read the sentences.
Then, write true, false, or
maybe on the lines.*

_____ 1. The teller gives Ms. Cruz $50.

_____ 2. Ms. Cruz spends $50 a week.

_____ 3. Ms. Cruz tears a check out of her checkbook.

_____ 4. She saves most of her money.

_____ 5. She only signs the check and not the deposit slip.

_____ 6. She gives the teller a receipt.

DESCRIPTIVE PHASE
Answer the following questions.

1. When does Ms. Cruz go to the bank?
2. How much money does Ms. Cruz keep for herself?
3. What does she write on the deposit slip first?
4. What does she sign?
5. Where does Ms. Cruz get the deposit slip?

ROLE PLAY
*Work with a partner. You play
one role. Your partner plays the
other role. Then, switch roles.*

Ms. Cruz: Hi, I want to deposit part of my paycheck.
Teller: How much is it for?
Ms. Cruz: It's for $300.
Teller: And how much do you want to deposit?
Ms. Cruz: Only $250.
Teller: Okay, put the check number here and the amount here.
Ms. Cruz: That seems easy enough.
Teller: Now, write $50 here in the "less cash" space.
Ms. Cruz: And now I just sign it?
Teller: Yes, that's it. Here's twenty, forty, fifty, and your receipt.

PAIR/GROUP WORK
*Ask your partner or group the
following questions.*

1. Do you deposit a check every Friday?
2. Do you get paid weekly, monthly, or bi-monthly?
3. What do you usually do with your paycheck?
4. How much cash do you get back?
5. What bank do you go to?
6. Do you like your bank? Why? Why not?

A Money Order from the Bank

Look at the illustrations. Listen carefully to your teacher.

70

PRESENTATION
Read the following sentences.

1. Mr. Chung's water bill this month is $47.
2. He asks his friend about money orders.
3. He goes down to the bank to get a money order.
4. He asks the teller for a $47 money order.
5. He gives the teller $47 and 50¢ for the money order.
6. He fills out the money order to the water district.
7. He tears off his receipt.
8. He puts the money order in the payment envelope.
9. He drops the envelope in the corner mailbox.

CONTROLLED PRACTICE
*Work with a partner.
One partner completes and
asks the questions. The other
partner answers.*

1. _____ much is Mr. Chung's water bill?

   _____ is $47.

2. _____ does he ask his friend about?

   _____ money orders.

3. _____ does he go down to the bank?

   _____ to get a money order.

4. Who does he _____ for a $47 money
   order?

   _____ the teller.

5. How _____ does he give the teller for
   the money order?

   _____ $47 and 50¢.

6. Who does he _____ out the money
   order to?

   _____ the water district.

7. What does he _____ off?

   _____ his receipt.

8. _____ does he put the money order?

   _____ in the payment envelope.

9. _____ does he drop the envelope?

   _____ in the corner mailbox.

COMPREHENSION

Complete these sentences. Write the correct letter on the lines.

_C_ 1. Mr. Chung _____ .   a. for a money order

_____ 2. Mr. Chung doesn't _____ .   b. costs 50 cents

_____ 3. Mr. Chung asks _____ .   c. has a water bill

_____ 4. The money order _____ .   d. $47.50

_____ 5. Mr. Chung pays _____ .   e. want to put cash in the mail

DESCRIPTIVE PHASE

Answer the following questions.

1. Whose water bill is $47?
2. Where does Mr. Chung buy a money order?
3. How much does he pay for the money order?
4. Who fills out the money order?
5. What does Mr. Chung keep?
6. What does he put in the payment envelope?

ROLE PLAY

Work with a partner. You play one role. Your partner plays the other role. Then, switch roles.

Mr. Chung: Hi, I need a money order.

Teller: All right. For what amount?

Mr. Chung: $47. It's for my water bill.

Teller: Okay, here's your money order.

Mr. Chung: Thanks. How much is the money order?

Teller: 50 cents. Your total is $47.50.

Mr. Chung: Okay. Where do I sign it?

Teller: At the bottom. Here.

Mr. Chung: And where do I put the payee's name?

Teller: Right here in the middle.

PAIR/GROUP WORK

Ask your partner or group the following questions.

1. Do you send money orders? For what?
2. Where can you buy a money order?
3. How much does a money order cost at the bank?
4. Why do you need a receipt for a money order?

Mail, Mail, Everywhere

Mailing a Letter

Look at the illustrations. Listen carefully to your teacher.

1. Andy is writing a letter to his wife in Taiwan.
2. He puts the letter in an envelope.
3. He licks the envelope and seals it.
4. He writes his return address in the upper left corner.
5. He writes her address in the middle.
6. He goes to the post office.
7. He puts coins in the stamp machine.
8. He pushes the button and a stamp comes out.
9. He puts the stamp on the upper right corner of the envelope and mails the letter.

CONTROLLED PRACTICE
*Work with a partner.
One partner completes and
asks the questions. The other
partner answers.*

1. What is Andy _____ ?
   _____ a letter to his wife.

2. _____ does he do with the letter?
   _____ puts the letter in an envelope.

3. _____ does he lick?
   _____ the envelope.

4. Where does he write his _____ ?
   _____ in the upper left corner.

5. What _____ he write in the middle?
   _____ her address.

6. _____ does he go?
   _____ to the post office.

7. Where does he _____ some coins?
   _____ in the stamp machine.

8. What _____ out?
   A stamp _____ .

9. Where _____ he put the stamp?
   _____ in the upper right corner.

COMPREHENSION

Read the sentences. Then, write true, false, or maybe on the lines.

_____ 1. Andy knows how to write.

_____ 2. Andy is sending money to his wife.

_____ 3. He writes two addresses on the envelope.

_____ 4. Andy doesn't have any stamps.

_____ 5. Andy buys stamps from a clerk.

_____ 6. Andy doesn't like to mail letters.

DESCRIPTIVE PHASE

Answer the following questions.

1. Where is Andy's wife?
2. What is Andy doing?
3. What does he do to the envelope?
4. Why does Andy go to the post office?
5. How does he get the stamp?
6. Where does he put the stamp?

ROLE PLAY

Work with a partner. You play one role. Your partner plays the other role. Then, switch roles.

Andy: I'm going to the post office. Need anything?

Son: No, nothing. Why don't you just go to the corner mailbox?

Andy: I can't. I need to buy a stamp.

Son: Do you need change?

Andy: No, I've got a dollar.

Son: Do they have change machines there?

Andy: Yes, next to the stamp machines.

Son: Why don't you buy a couple extra stamps?

Andy: Maybe I will.

PAIR/GROUP WORK

Ask your partner or group the following questions.

1. How far is the post office from your house?
2. What street is your post office on?
3. What time does the post office open in the morning?
4. What time does it close?
5. Is there a change machine there?
6. How often do you write letters?
7. How much does it cost to send a letter to your country?

Postal Money Order

Look at the illustrations. Listen carefully to your teacher.

Read the following sentences.

1. Ms. Smith needs to mail her telephone payment.
2. She has cash but no checks.
3. She goes to the post office.
4. She tells the clerk she needs a money order for $23.
5. She pays him for the money order.
6. She writes *Telecom* in the payee space.
7. She signs her name.
8. She tears off the stub and puts it in her purse.
9. She puts the money order in the payment envelope.

CONTROLLED PRACTICE
*Work with a partner.
One partner completes and
asks the questions. The other
partner answers.*

1. What does Ms. Smith _____ to mail?

   _____ her telephone payment.

2. Does she have cash or _____ ?

   _____ cash.

3. _____ does she go?

   _____ to the post office.

4. What does she tell the _____ ?

   _____ a money order for $23.

5. _____ does she pay him for?

   _____ the money order.

6. Where _____ she write *Telecom*?

   _____ in the payee space.

7. Then, _____ does she do?

   _____ signs her name.

8. Where does she _____ the stub?

   _____ in her purse.

9. Where does she put the _____ order?

   _____ in the payment envelope.

COMPREHENSION

Complete these sentences. Write the correct letter on the lines.

_C_	1.	Ms. Smith doesn't _____.	a. a money order
____	2.	Ms. Smith wants _____.	b. her name
____	3.	Ms. Smith signs _____.	c. have checks
____	4.	Her telephone bill _____.	d. is for $23
____	5.	She keeps _____.	e. the stub

DESCRIPTIVE PHASE

Answer the following questions.

1. Who needs to pay her telephone bill?
2. How does she pay?
3. Where does she buy her money order?
4. How much is the money order for?
5. What does she write in the payee space?
6. What does she keep?

ROLE PLAY

Work with a partner. You play one role. Your partner plays the other role. Then, switch roles.

Ms. Smith:	Hi, can I buy a money order here?
Clerk:	Sure, for how much?
Ms. Smith:	For $23.
Clerk:	Here you go. That's $24.75.
Ms. Smith:	Okay, here's $24.75. Where do I write the payee's name?
Clerk:	Right here. And you sign here.
Ms. Smith:	Which part do I keep?
Clerk:	This part. It's the stub.
Ms. Smith:	And I mail this part?
Clerk:	That's right. You've got it.

PAIR/GROUP WORK

Ask your partner or group the following questions.

1. Do you buy money orders? Why? Why not?
2. How much do money orders cost at the post office?
3. Why don't you put cash in the mail?
4. Do you keep the stub from your money orders? Why? Why not?

Change of Address

Look at the illustrations. Listen carefully to your teacher.

PRESENTATION

Read the following sentences.

1. Ms. Ma is moving from New York to California.
2. She asks the postal clerk for a change of address form.
3. The clerk gives her a form.
4. Ms. Ma takes it home.
5. She reads the directions.
6. She prints her old address first.
7. She prints her new address under her old address.
8. She signs it at the bottom.
9. She goes to the mailbox and drops it in.

CONTROLLED PRACTICE

*Work with a partner.
One partner completes and
asks the questions. The other
partner answers.*

1. Who is _____ from New York?

   Ms. Ma _____ .

2. What does she _____ the postal clerk for?

   _____ for a change of address form.

3. Who gives her a _____ ?

   The clerk _____ .

4. _____ does Ms. Ma take it?

   _____ home.

5. What does she _____ ?

   _____ the directions.

6. Which address does she _____ first?

   _____ her old address.

7. Where does she print _____ new address?

   _____ under her old address.

8. Where does she _____ the form?

   _____ at the bottom.

9. Where does she _____ ?

   _____ to the mailbox.

COMPREHENSION

Read the sentences. Then, write true, false, or maybe on the lines.

_____ 1. Ms. Ma is moving from California to New York.

_____ 2. She doesn't like New York.

_____ 3. Ms. Ma fills out the form at the post office.

_____ 4. Ms. Ma doesn't know her old address.

_____ 5. The clerk signs the change of address form.

_____ 6. Ms. Ma mails the change of address form.

DESCRIPTIVE PHASE

Answer the following questions.

1. Where is Ms. Ma going?
2. What does she get at the post office?
3. Where does she take the form?
4. What two things does she print?
5. Where does she sign the form?

ROLE PLAY

Work with a partner. You play one role. Your partner plays the other role. Then, switch roles.

Ms. Ma:	Hi, could you help me?
Postal clerk:	Sure, what do you need?
Ms. Ma:	I need a change of address form.
Postal clerk:	Here you are.
Ms. Ma:	How do I fill this out?
Postal clerk:	Print your old address here and your new one here.
Ms. Ma:	Is that it?
Postal clerk:	Almost. Now sign it here.
Ms. Ma:	Do I mail it or give it to you?
Postal clerk:	You can just give it to me.

PAIR/GROUP WORK

Ask your partner or group the following questions.

1. What's your current address?
2. What was your previous address?
3. When do you fill out a change of address form?
4. Where is the closest mailbox to your house?
5. Do you change addresses often?

A Certified Letter

Look at the illustrations. Listen carefully to your teacher.

82

PRESENTATION

Read the following sentences.

1. Ms. Silva is watching TV.
2. She hears a knock on the door.
3. She looks through the peephole in the door.
4. The mail carrier gives her a certified letter.
5. Ms. Silva signs the return receipt.
6. The mail carrier tears off the return receipt.
7. She takes the letter inside and opens it.
8. The letter is from her car insurance company.
9. The mail carrier takes the return receipt back to the post office.

CONTROLLED PRACTICE

Work with a partner. One partner completes and asks the questions. The other partner answers.

1. Who is _____ TV in her living room?

   Ms. Silva _____ .

2. What _____ she hear?

   _____ a knock on the door.

3. What does she _____ through?

   _____ the peephole.

4. What does the _____ give her?

   _____ a certified letter.

5. Who _____ the return receipt?

   Ms. Silva _____ .

6. Who _____ off the return receipt?

   The mail carrier _____ .

7. _____ does she take the letter?

   _____ inside.

8. _____ is the letter from?

   _____ her insurance company.

9. What does the _____ do with the receipt?

   _____ takes the return receipt back to the post office.

1. Ms. Silva is reading the newspaper in her living room.

   No, she isn't.

2. Ms. Silva isn't careful.

   _____

3. The mail carrier gives her a package.

   _____

DESCRIPTIVE PHASE

Answer the following questions.

1. What is Ms. Silva doing?
2. Who knocks at her door?
3. What kind of letter does the mail carrier give her?
4. Who signs the return receipt?
5. Who is the letter from?
6. Who keeps the return receipt?

ROLE PLAY

*Work with a partner. You play
one role. Your partner plays the
other role. Then, switch roles.*

Mail carrier:	Hello, I need to get your signature.
Ms. Silva:	My signature. What for?
Mail carrier:	You have a certified letter.
Ms. Silva:	What's that?
Mail carrier:	It's a letter with a receipt.
Ms. Silva:	Who's it from?
Mail carrier:	I don't know.
Ms. Silva:	Do I need to pay any money?
Mail carrier:	Oh no, all you do is sign.
Ms. Silva:	Okay, where?

PAIR/GROUP WORK

*Ask your partner or group the
following questions.*

1. Do you get certified letters?
2. Why do people send certified letters?
3. Do you send certified letters?
4. How much does it cost to send a certified letter?
5. Do you keep your return receipt?

Eating Out

A Special Occasion

Look at the illustrations. Listen carefully to your teacher.

PRESENTATION
Read the following sentences.

1. Raymond and Sylvia are going out for dinner.
2. Raymond tells the hostess that they are a party of two.
3. The hostess asks him if he wants smoking or non-smoking.
4. Raymond says, "non-smoking."
5. The hostess seats them and gives them their menus.
6. The waiter comes to take their orders.
7. Sylvia orders lobster and a baked potato.
8. Raymond orders a steak and French fries.
9. They both go to the salad bar.

CONTROLLED PRACTICE
Work with a partner. One partner completes and asks the questions. The other partner answers.

1. _____ are Raymond and Sylvia going?
   _____ out for dinner.
2. What does Raymond _____ the hostess?
   _____ that they are a party of two.
3. What does the _____ ask him?
   _____ if he wants smoking or non-smoking.
4. What does Raymond _____ ?
   _____ , "non-smoking."
5. What _____ the hostess give them?
   _____ their menus.
6. Who _____ their orders?
   _____ takes their orders.
7. _____ does Sylvia order?
   _____ lobster and a baked potato.
8. What does Raymond _____ ?
   _____ a steak and French fries.
9. _____ do they both go?
   _____ to the salad bar.

COMPREHENSION

Read the sentences. Then, write true, false, or maybe on the lines.

_____ 1. Raymond and Sylvia are hungry.

_____ 2. Raymond and Sylvia are married.

_____ 3. Sylvia orders steak and a baked potato.

_____ 4. There are smoking sections at the restaurant.

_____ 5. The waiter gives them menus.

_____ 6. The hostess takes their orders.

DESCRIPTIVE PHASE

Answer the following questions.

1. How many people are in Raymond's party?
2. Who asks Raymond if he wants smoking or non-smoking?
3. Who seats Raymond and Sylvia?
4. What section does Raymond choose?
5. Who takes their order?
6. What do they both do after they order?

ROLE PLAY

Work with a partner. You play one role. Your partner plays the other role. Then, switch roles.

Waiter: Good evening, folks. Have you decided?
Raymond: Yes, I'd like the steak with fries.
Waiter: And how would you like that cooked?
Raymond: Medium.
Waiter: And how about you, ma'am?
Sylvia: I'd like the lobster and a baked potato.
Waiter: Butter, sour cream, and chives on that?
Sylvia: No, just butter.
Waiter: Anything to drink?
Raymond: Yes, I'd like coffee, black.
Sylvia: I'd like coffee with cream and sugar.

PAIR/GROUP WORK

Ask your partner or group the following questions.

1. How do you like your steak cooked?
2. Do you sit in the smoking or non-smoking section?
3. Do you like baked potatoes?
4. What do you put on your baked potato?
5. How do you take your coffee?
6. What kind of dressing do you like on your salad?

Using a Coupon

Look at the illustrations. Listen carefully to your teacher.

PRESENTATION

Read the following sentences.

1. Gilberto is reading the newspaper.
2. There's a coupon for pizza.
3. He can get two pizzas for the price of one.
4. He cuts out the coupon and puts it in his wallet.
5. He goes down to the pizza restaurant.
6. He gives the coupon to the cashier.
7. He orders two large pizzas to go.
8. The cashier charges him for one.
9. Twenty minutes later, he takes the pizzas home.

CONTROLLED PRACTICE

Work with a partner. One partner completes and asks the questions. The other partner answers.

1. Who is _____ the newspaper?

   Gilberto _____ .

2. What is the _____ for?

   _____ pizza.

3. How _____ pizzas can he get for the price of one?

   _____ two pizzas

   _____ .

4. _____ does he put the coupon?

   _____ in his wallet.

5. Where _____ he go?

   _____ down to the pizza restaurant.

6. Who _____ he give the coupon to?

   _____ the cashier.

7. How many _____ does he order?

   _____ two large pizzas.

8. How many does the cashier _____ him for?

   _____ one.

9. _____ does he take the pizzas home?

   _____ later.

COMPREHENSION

Complete the second line of these dialogues.

1. Gilberto: Let's get a pizza for dinner.

   Maria: *That's a good idea.*

2. Gilberto: The pizza is on special.

   Maria: _____

3. Gilberto: What do you want on your pizza?

   Maria: _____

DESCRIPTIVE PHASE

Answer the following questions.

1. What is Gilberto doing?
2. What does he cut out from the newspaper?
3. What does he give to the cashier?
4. What size pizza does he order?
5. Where does he take the pizzas?

ROLE PLAY

Work with a partner. You play one role. Your partner plays the other role. Then, switch roles.

Cashier: Hi, can I help you?

Gilberto: Sure, I'd like two pizzas to go.

Cashier: What did you want on those?

Gilberto: Just mushrooms.

Cashier: Okay, and what size pizzas?

Gilberto: Large.

Cashier: Do you have any coupons?

Gilberto: Yeah. Here, it's a two-for-one coupon.

Cashier: So your total will be $11.65.

Gilberto: Here's $20.

PAIR/GROUP WORK

Ask your partner or group the following questions.

1. Do you use coupons? For what?
2. Where can you get coupons?
3. Why do you use coupons?
4. What is your favorite kind of pizza?
5. Where do you prefer to eat your pizza?

A Hamburger for Lunch

Look at the illustrations. Listen carefully to your teacher.

1. Alfredo wants a hamburger for lunch.
2. He pulls into the drive-through lane of a fast-food restaurant.
3. He drives up to the outside menu.
4. The voice from the speaker asks for his order.
5. He orders a burger, a coke, and a small fry.
6. Then, he drives up to the pick-up window.
7. The cashier tells him how much to pay.
8. Alfredo pays the cashier.
9. The cashier gives him his change and his food.

CONTROLLED PRACTICE
Work with a partner.
One partner completes and
asks the questions. The other
partner answers.

1. What _____ Alfredo want for lunch?

   _____ a hamburger.

2. _____ does he pull into?

   _____ the drive-through lane of a fast-

   food restaurant.

3. What does he _____ up to?

   _____ the outside menu.

4. What does the voice from the speaker

   _____ ?

   _____ for his order.

5. What does he _____ ?

   _____ a burger, a coke, and a small fry.

6. Then, _____ does he do?

   _____ up to the pick-up window.

7. _____ does the cashier tell him?

   _____ how much to pay.

8. Who does Alfredo _____ ?

   _____ the cashier.

9. What does the _____ give Alfredo?

   _____ his change and his food.

COMPREHENSION
*Read the sentences.
Then, write true, false, or
maybe on the lines.*

_____ 1. Alfredo likes hamburgers.

_____ 2. Alfredo orders two hamburgers.

_____ 3. Alfredo is hungry.

_____ 4. Alfredo orders coffee.

_____ 5. Alfredo goes inside the restaurant.

_____ 6. Alfredo orders a coke.

DESCRIPTIVE PHASE
Answer the following questions.

1. What does Alfredo want for lunch?
2. What kind of restaurant does he go to?
3. Does he go inside or to the drive-through?
4. Where does Alfredo pay for his lunch?
5. What does Alfredo order?
6. Who gives him his food?

ROLE PLAY
*Work with a partner. You play
one role. Your partner plays the
other role. Then, switch roles.*

Speaker: Hello, may I take your order?
Alfredo: Sure, I'd like a hamburger, an order of fries, and a
           coke.
Speaker: What size fries?
Alfredo: Medium.
Speaker: What size drink?
Alfredo: Make it a large.
Speaker: Anything else?
Alfredo: No, that's it.
Speaker: Okay, your total is $3.49.

PAIR/GROUP WORK
*Ask your partner or group the
following questions.*

1. What do you eat for lunch?
2. Do you eat hamburgers? Why? Why not?
3. Do you like French fries?
4. Do you use the drive-through lane? Why? Why not?

Ice Cream

Look at the illustrations. Listen carefully to your teacher.

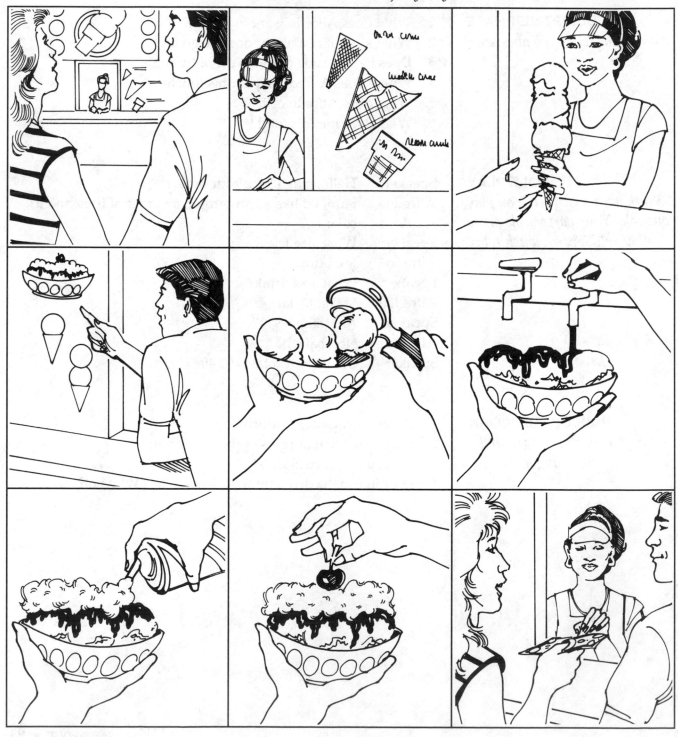

94

1. Tom and Gloria are going to get ice cream.
2. They have sugar cones, waffle cones, and plain cones.
3. Gloria orders a triple vanilla on a sugar cone.
4. Tom wants a hot fudge sundae.
5. The cashier puts three scoops of ice cream in a cup.
6. Then, she puts some hot fudge on top.
7. She sprays whipped cream all over.
8. She puts a cherry on top.
9. Gloria pays for her's and Tom's ice cream.

CONTROLLED PRACTICE
*Work with a partner.
One partner completes and
asks the questions. The other
partner answers.*

1. What _____ Tom and Gloria going to get?

_____ ice cream.

2. What _____ of cones do they have?

_____ sugar cones, waffle cones, and plain cones.

3. What _____ Gloria order?

_____ a triple vanilla on a sugar cone.

4. _____ does Tom want?

_____ a hot fudge sundae.

5. How many _____ does the cashier put in a cup?

_____ three scoops

_____ .

6. _____ does she put the hot fudge?

_____ on top.

7. What does she _____ all over?

_____ whipped cream

_____ .

8. _____ does she put a cherry?

_____ on top.

9. _____ pays for the ice cream?

Gloria _____ .

1. There are two kinds of cones.
   No, there aren't.

2. Gloria gets one scoop of ice cream.

3. The cashier puts Tom's ice cream on a sugar cone.

DESCRIPTIVE PHASE
Answer the following questions.

1. Who is with Gloria?
2. What are they going to do?
3. How many kinds of cones do they have?
4. What kind of cone does Gloria get?
5. What does the cashier put on Tom's ice cream?
6. Who pays for the ice cream?

ROLE PLAY
Work with a partner. You play one role. Your partner plays the other role. Then, switch roles.

Cashier: Hi, can I help you?
Gloria: Sure, I want a triple vanilla.
Cashier: On what kind of cone?
Gloria: A sugar cone, please.
Cashier: And how about you, sir?
Tom: I'd like a hot fudge sundae.
Cashier: Whipped cream, nuts, and a cherry?
Tom: Yes, give me the works.
Cashier: Anything else for you tonight?
Tom: No, that should do it.

PAIR/GROUP WORK
Ask your partner or group the following questions.

1. What's your favorite flavor of ice cream?
2. What kind of cone do you usually get?
3. How many scoops can you eat?
4. Do you like hot fudge sundaes?
5. How much does a single cone usually cost?

Answer Key

Unit 1 — Do You Have a Problem?

A Fire

COMPREHENSION

1. false   2. false   3. false   4. true   5. false

DESCRIPTIVE PHASE

1. in their room
2. sleeping
3. Luis
4. Luis's neighbor

A Prowler

DESCRIPTIVE PHASE

1. through a window
2. one
3. The prowler knocks over a lamp.
4. Alfredo
5. the police
6. to get away

Noisy Neighbor

COMPREHENSION

2. d   3. a   4. b   5. c

DESCRIPTIVE PHASE

1. She is angry because her neighbor is having a loud party.
2. to ask her to be quiet
3. to be quiet
4. because her neighbor makes more noise
5. They talk to her neighbor.

Speeding

COMPREHENSION

1. false   2. true   3. maybe   4. true
5. maybe   6. true

DESCRIPTIVE PHASE

1. 45 miles per hour
2. 25 miles per hour
3. his license and car registration
4. his ticket book
5. Jaime

Unit 2 — Take Care of Yourself

At the Dentist

COMPREHENSION

2. c   3. a   4. d   5. b

DESCRIPTIVE PHASE

1. She has a bad toothache.
2. at the dentist's office
3. a medical history form
4. at the bottom
5. on the medical history form

A Burn

COMPREHENSION

1. maybe   2. false   3. false   4. true   5. true

DESCRIPTIVE PHASE

1. cooking dinner
2. He burns his hand.
3. He sticks his son's hand under cold water.
4. He rubs it into his son's hand.
5. He puts it on his son's hand.

Cough and Fever

DESCRIPTIVE PHASE

1. He is coughing a lot.
2. She feels his forehead.
3. 102 degrees
4. She shakes it a couple of times. She puts it in Doug's mouth.
5. two aspirins

Twisted Ankle

COMPREHENSION

2. Yes, he does.   3. No, she doesn't.   4. No, he doesn't.   5. No, she doesn't.   6. No, she doesn't.

DESCRIPTIVE PHASE

1. He twists his ankle.
2. his sister
3. the nurse
4. He examines Sergio's ankle.
5. He gives Sergio some crutches.

Unit 3 — You Are What You Eat

Sugar and Salt

COMPREHENSION

2. c   3. a   4. b   5. e

DESCRIPTIVE PHASE

1. her son
2. to put the box of cereal back
3. lots of sugar and salt
4. because it contains lots of sugar and salt
5. Ms. Baker

Getting a Rain Check

COMPREHENSION

2. No, she doesn't.   3. No, it isn't.   4. No, it doesn't.   5. Yes, she does.   6. Yes, she can.

DESCRIPTIVE PHASE

1. reading the newspaper
2. in the newspaper
3. Yes, for half-price.
4. the ad
5. next week

Paying with a Check

DESCRIPTIVE PHASE

1. to the checkout lane
2. groceries
3. with a check
4. her license and a credit card
5. her license and credit card numbers
6. paper

The Expiration Date

COMPREHENSION

1. maybe   2. false   3. maybe   4. true   5. maybe   6. false

DESCRIPTIVE PHASE

1. at the corner market
2. two cartons
3. less than five dollars
4. cash
5. his change and receipt

Unit 4 — If It Fits, Wear It

Shoes for Everyone

DESCRIPTIVE PHASE

1. tennis shoes
2. into the back room
3. yes
4. in the boxes
5. with his credit card
6. on the slip

Returning Merchandise

DESCRIPTIVE PHASE

1. her husband
2. no
3. It's much too big.
4. She takes the coat back to the store.
5. the salesclerk
6. an exchange

Make Sure Your Pants Fit

COMPREHENSION

1. true   2. false   3. false   4. true   5. false   6. false

DESCRIPTIVE PHASE

1. Roberto
2. his waist and inseam
3. a rack of pants that are his size
4. in the dressing room
5. He takes off the new pants.
6. one pair

Buying a Shirt

COMPREHENSION

2. No, he doesn't.   3. No, he doesn't.   4. No, he doesn't.   5. Yes, he does.   6. Yes, he does.

DESCRIPTIVE PHASE

1. on the rack
2. 17 inches
3. the regular-fit and the tapered shirts
4. the regular-fit shirts
5. It doesn't fit.

Unit 5 — Do You Have Wheels?

Overheating

COMPREHENSION

1. false 2. maybe 3. false 4. true 5. false
6. false

DESCRIPTIVE PHASE

1. to work
2. on the dashboard
3. His car is running very hot.
4. the station attendant
5. He pours cold water on it.

Changing a Flat

COMPREHENSION

2. a 3. f 4. b 5. c 6. d

DESCRIPTIVE PHASE

1. to the park
2. The tire goes flat.
3. Toshi
4. from the trunk
5. He unscrews the lug bolts.

Oil Change

COMPREHENSION

1. false 2. false 3. maybe 4. true 5. false

DESCRIPTIVE PHASE

1. to the mechanic
2. to get the oil changed
3. the work order
4. the mechanic
5. the bolt
6. some new oil

Alignment

COMPREHENSION

2. No, she doesn't. 3. Yes, she does.

DESCRIPTIVE PHASE

1. the front tires aren't straight
2. up on a rack
3. that she needs a front-end alignment
4. the work order
5. in the waiting room

Unit 6 — Banking

Opening an Account

COMPREHENSION

1. false 2. true 3. false 4. maybe 5. true

DESCRIPTIVE PHASE

1. at the bank
2. open a checking account
3. the "New Accounts" clerk
4. a book of check designs
5. a check design

Using the ATM

COMPREHENSION

2. No, she doesn't. 3. No, she doesn't.
4. Yes, she does. 5. No, she doesn't.

DESCRIPTIVE PHASE

1. She needs some money.
2. her bank card
3. her secret code
4. to withdraw cash
5. $100

Deposit with Cash Back

COMPREHENSION

1. true 2. maybe 3. false 4. maybe 5. false
6. false

DESCRIPTIVE PHASE

1. every Friday
2. $50
3. the check number
4. the deposit slip
5. from her checkbook

A Money Order from the Bank

COMPREHENSION

2. e 3. a 4. b 5. d

DESCRIPTIVE PHASE

1. Mr. Chung's
2. at the bank
3. 50¢
4. Mr. Chung
5. his receipt
6. the money order

Unit 7 — Mail, Mail, Everywhere

Mailing a Letter

COMPREHENSION
1. true 2. false 3. true 4. true 5. false
6. maybe

DESCRIPTIVE PHASE
1. in Taiwan
2. writing a letter
3. He licks it and seals it.
4. to buy a stamp
5. from a stamp machine
6. on the upper right corner of the envelope

Postal Money Order

COMPREHENSION
2. a 3. b 4. d 5. e

DESCRIPTIVE PHASE
1. Ms. Smith
2. with a money order
3. at the post office
4. $23
5. *Telecom*
6. the stub

Change of Address

COMPREHENSION
1. false 2. maybe 3. false 4. false 5. false
6. true

DESCRIPTIVE PHASE
1. to California
2. a change of address form
3. home
4. her old address and her new address
5. at the bottom

A Certified Letter

COMPREHENSION
2. Yes, she is. 3. No, he doesn't.

DESCRIPTIVE PHASE
1. watching TV
2. the mail carrier
3. a certified letter
4. Ms. Silva
5. her insurance company
6. the mail carrier

Unit 8 — Eating Out

A Special Occasion

COMPREHENSION
1. true 2. maybe 3. false 4. true 5. false
6. false

DESCRIPTIVE PHASE
1. two
2. the hostess
3. the hostess
4. non-smoking
5. the waiter
6. They go to the salad bar.

Using a Coupon

DESCRIPTIVE PHASE
1. reading the newspaper
2. a coupon for pizza
3. the coupon
4. large
5. home

A Hamburger for Lunch

COMPREHENSION
1. true 2. false 3. true 4. false 5. false
6. true

DESCRIPTIVE PHASE
1. a hamburger
2. a fast-food restaurant
3. to the drive-through lane
4. at the pick-up window
5. a hamburger, a coke, and a small fry
6. the cashier

Ice Cream

COMPREHENSION
2. No, she doesn't. 3. No, she doesn't.

DESCRIPTIVE PHASE
1. Tom
2. get ice cream
3. three
4. a sugar cone
5. hot fudge, whipped cream, and a cherry
6. Gloria